Coaching
Youth Basketball

Third Edition

American Sport Education Program

Human Kinetics

Library of Congress Cataloging-in-Publication Data

Coaching youth basketball / American Sport Education Program--3rd ed.
   p. cm.
   ISBN 0-7360-3715-2
   1. Basketball for children--Coaching. 2. Basketball--Coaching. I. American Sport Education Program.

   GV885.3.C63 2001
   796.323'07'7--dc21   2001016656

ISBN: 0-7360-3715-2

Material in chapters 4 and 6 is reprinted, by permission, from YMCA of the USA, 1999, *Coaching YMCA Winners Baseball and Softball* (Champaign, IL: Human Kinetics).

Acquisitions Editor: Thomas Hanlon; **Games Consultant**: Kelly Valentino; **Managing Editor**: Wendy McLaughlin; **Assistant Editor**: Dan Brachtesende; **Copyeditor**: Jan Feeney; **Proofreader**: Sue Fetters; **Graphic Designer**: Fred Starbird; **Graphic Artist**: Dody Bullerman and Yvonne Griffith; **Photo Manager:** Gayle Garrison; **Cover Designer**: Jack Davis; **Photographer (cover)**: Tom Roberts; **Photographer (interior)**: Tom Roberts; photos pp. 1, 9, 17, 39, 51, 63 © Terry Wild, photos pp. 33, 75, 145 © Bruce Coleman; **Art Manager**: Craig Newsom; **Illustrator**: Tom Janowski; **Printer**: United Graphics

Copies of this book are available at special discounts for bulk purchase for sales promotions, premiums, fund-raising, or educational use. Special editions or book excerpts can also be created to specifications. For details, contact the Special Sales Manager at Human Kinetics.

Printed in the United States of America   10 9 8 7 6 5 4 3 2 1

Human Kinetics
Web site: www.humankinetics.com

United States: Human Kinetics
P.O. Box 5076
Champaign, IL 61825-5076
800-747-4457
e-mail: humank@hkusa.com

Canada: Human Kinetics
475 Devonshire Road Unit 100
Windsor, ON N8Y 2L5
800-465-7301 (in Canada only)
e-mail: orders@hkcanada.com

Europe: Human Kinetics
Units C2/C3 Wira Business Park
West Park Ring Road
Leeds LS16 6EB, United Kingdom
+44 (0) 113 278 1708
e-mail: hk@hkeurope.com

Australia: Human Kinetics
57A Price Avenue
Lower Mitcham, South Australia 5062
08 8277 1555
e-mail: liahka@senet.com.au

New Zealand: Human Kinetics
P.O. Box 105-231, Auckland Central
09-523-3462
e-mail: hkp@ihug.co.nz

Contents

Welcome to Coaching!

Coaching young people is an exciting way to be involved in sport. But it isn't easy. Some coaches are overwhelmed by the responsibilities involved in helping athletes through their early sport experiences. And that's not surprising, because coaching youngsters requires more than bringing the ball to the court and letting the team play. It involves preparing players physically and mentally to compete effectively, fairly, and safely in their sport, and providing them with a positive role model.

This book will help you meet the challenges *and* experience the many rewards of coaching young athletes. In this book you'll learn how to meet your responsibilities as a coach, to communicate well and provide for safety, to use a highly effective method—the games approach—to teach tactics and skills, and to apply strategies for coaching on game day. We also provide three sets of season plans to guide you throughout your season.

This book serves as a text for the American Sport Education Program's Coaching Youth Sport course. If you would like more information about this course or other ASEP courses and resources, please contact us at

ASEP
P.O. Box 5076
Champaign, IL 61825-5076
1-800-747-5698
www.asep.com

Key to Diagrams

player with ball	Ⓞ
offensive player	O
defensive player	X
coach	C
pass	- - - - -→
dribble	∿∿∿→
move	——→
shoot	·········→
screen or box out	——⊣

chapter 1

Stepping Into Coaching

If you are like most youth league coaches, you have probably been recruited from the ranks of concerned parents, sport enthusiasts, or community volunteers. Like many rookie and veteran coaches, you probably have had little formal instruction on how to coach. But when the call went out for coaches to assist with the local youth basketball program, you answered because you like children and enjoy basketball, and perhaps because you wanted to be involved in a worthwhile community activity.

Your initial coaching assignment may be difficult. Like many volunteers, you may not know everything there is to know about basketball or about how to work with children. *Coaching Youth Basketball* will help you learn the basics of coaching basketball effectively.

To start, let's take a look at what's involved in being a coach. What are your responsibilities? We'll also talk about how to handle the situation when your child is on the team you coach, and we'll examine five tools for being an effective coach.

Your Responsibilities As a Coach

As a basketball coach, you'll be called upon to do the following:

1. **Provide a safe physical environment.** Playing basketball holds an inherent risk, but as a coach you're responsible for regularly inspecting the practice and competition courts (see the checklist for facilities and equipment in chapter 6).

2. **Communicate in a positive way.** You'll communicate not only with your players but also with parents, referees, and administrators. Communicate in a way that is positive and that demonstrates you have the best interests of the players at heart. Chapter 2 will help you communicate effectively and positively.

3. **Teach the tactics and skills of basketball.** We'll show you an innovative "games approach" to teaching and practicing the tactics and skills young athletes need to know—an approach that kids thoroughly enjoy. We ask you to help all players be the best they can be. In chapter 5 we'll show you how to teach basketball skills, and in chapter 9 we'll provide season plans for 8- to 9-year-olds, 10- to 11-year-olds, and 12- to 14-year-olds, respectively. In chapter 8 we'll provide descriptions of all the tactics and skills you'll need to teach and to help you detect and correct errors that players typically make.

4. **Teach the rules of basketball.** We'll ask you to teach your players the rules of basketball. You'll find the rules in chapter 7.

5. **Direct players in competition.** This includes determining starting lineups and a substitution plan, relating appropriately to referees and to opposing coaches and players, and making tactical decisions during games (see chapter 6). Remember that the focus is not on winning at all costs, but in coaching your kids to compete well, do their best, and strive to win within the rules.

6. **Help your players become fit and value fitness for a lifetime.** We want you to help your players be fit so they can play basketball safely and successfully. We also want your players to learn to become fit on their own, understand the value of fitness, and enjoy training. Thus, we ask you not to make them do push-ups or run laps for punishment. Make it fun to get fit for basketball, and make it fun to play basketball so they'll stay fit for a lifetime.

7. **Help young people develop character.** Character development includes learning caring, honesty, respect, and responsibility. These intangible qualities are no less important to teach than the skill of shooting the ball well. We ask you to teach these values to players both by conducting Team Circles after every game and by demonstrating and encouraging behaviors that express these values at all times.

These are your responsibilities as a coach. But coaching becomes even more complicated when your child is a player on the team you coach. If this is the case, you'll have to take into account your roles as both a coach and a parent, and think about how those roles relate to each other.

Coaching Your Own Child

Many coaches are parents, but the two roles should not be confused. Unlike your role as a parent, as a coach you are responsible not only to yourself and your child, but also to the organization, all the players on the team (including your child), and their parents. Because of this additional responsibility, your behavior on the basketball court will be different from your behavior at home, and your son or daughter may not understand why.

For example, imagine the confusion of a young boy who is the center of his parents' attention at home but is barely noticed by his father/coach in the sport setting. Or consider the mixed signals received by a young girl whose basketball skill is constantly evaluated by a mother/coach who otherwise rarely comments on her daughter's activities. You need to explain to your son or daughter your new responsibilities and how they will affect your relationship when coaching.

Take the following steps to avoid problems in coaching your child:

⊙ Ask your child if he or she wants you to coach the team.
⊙ Explain why you wish to be involved with the team.
⊙ Discuss with your child how your interactions will change when you take on the role of coach at practices or games.
⊙ Limit your coaching behavior to when you are in the coaching role.
⊙ Avoid parenting during practice or game situations, to keep your role clear in your child's mind.
⊙ Reaffirm your love for your child, irrespective of his or her performance on the basketball court.

Now let's look at some of the qualities that will help you become an effective coach.

Five Tools of an Effective Coach

Have you purchased the traditional coaching tools—things like whistles, coaching clothes, sport shoes, and a clipboard? They'll help you coach, but to be a successful coach you'll need five other tools that cannot be bought. These tools are available only through self-examination and hard work; they're easy to remember with the acronym COACH:

C – Comprehension

O – Outlook

A – Affection

C – Character

H – Humor

Comprehension

Comprehension of the rules, tactics, and skills of basketball is required. You must understand the basic elements of the sport. To assist you in learning about the game, we describe rules, tactics, and skills in chapters 7 and 8. We also provide season plans in chapter 9.

To improve your comprehension of basketball, take the following steps:

- Read the sport-specific section of this book in chapters 7, 8, and 9.
- Consider reading other basketball coaching books, including those available from the American Sport Education Program (ASEP).
- Contact youth basketball organizations.
- Attend basketball clinics.
- Talk with more experienced coaches.
- Observe local college, high school, and youth basketball games.
- Watch basketball games on television.

In addition to having basketball knowledge, you must implement proper training and safety methods so your players can participate with little risk of injury. Even then, injuries may occur. And more often than not, you'll be the first person responding to your players' injuries, so be sure you understand the basic emergency care procedures described in chapter 3. Also, read in that chapter how to handle more serious sport injury situations.

Outlook

This coaching tool refers to your perspective and goals—what you are seeking as a coach. The most common coaching objectives are to (a) have fun, (b) help players develop their physical, mental, and social skills, and (c) win. Thus your *outlook* involves the priorities you set, your planning, and your vision for the future.

While all coaches focus on competition, we want you to focus on *positive* competition, keeping the pursuit of victory in perspective by making decisions that first are in the best interest of the players, and second will help to win the game.

So how do you know if your outlook and priorities are in order? Here's a little test for you:

Which situation would you be most proud of?

    a. Knowing that each participant enjoyed playing basketball.

    b. Seeing that all players improved their basketball skills.

    c. Winning the league championship.

Which statement best reflects your thoughts about sport?

    a. If it isn't fun, don't do it.

    b. Everyone should learn something every day.

    c. Sport isn't fun if you don't win.

How would you like your players to remember you?

    a. As a coach who was fun to play for.

    b. As a coach who provided a good base of fundamental skills.

    c. As a coach who had a winning record.

Which would you most like to hear a parent of a player on your team say?

    a. Mike really had a good time playing basketball this year.

    b. Nicole learned some important lessons playing basketball this year.

    c. Willie played on the first-place basketball team this year.

Which of the following would be the most rewarding moment of your season?

    a. Having your team not want to stop playing, even after practice is over.

    b. Seeing one of your players finally master the skill of dribbling without constantly looking at the ball.

    c. Winning the league championship.

Look over your answers. If you most often selected "a" responses, then having fun is most important to you. A majority of "b" answers suggests that skill development is what attracts you to coaching. And if "c" was your most frequent response, winning is tops on your list of coaching priorities. If your priorities are in order, your players' well-being will take precedence over your team's win-loss record every time.

The American Sport Education Program (ASEP) has a motto that will help you keep your outlook in line with the best interests of the kids on your team. It summarizes in four words all you need to remember when establishing your coaching priorities:

Athletes First, Winning Second

This motto recognizes that striving to win is an important, even vital, part of sports. But it emphatically states that no efforts in striving to win should be made at the expense of the athletes' well-being, development, and enjoyment.

Take the following actions to better define your outlook:

1. Determine your priorities for the season.
2. Prepare for situations that challenge your priorities.
3. Set goals for yourself and your players that are consistent with those priorities.
4. Plan how you and your players can best attain those goals.
5. Review your goals frequently to be sure that you are staying on track.

Affection

This is another vital tool you will want to have in your coaching kit: a genuine concern for the young people you coach. It involves having a love for kids, a desire to share with them your love and knowledge of basketball, and the patience and understanding that allow each individual playing for you to grow from his or her involvement in sport.

You can demonstrate your affection and patience in many ways, including these:

- Make an effort to get to know each player on your team.
- Treat each player as an individual.
- Empathize with players trying to learn new and difficult skills.
- Treat players as you would like to be treated under similar circumstances.
- Be in control of your emotions.

◎ Show your enthusiasm for being involved with your team.

◎ Keep an upbeat and positive tone in all of your communications.

Character

The fact that you have decided to coach young basketball players probably means that you think participation in sport is important. But whether or not that participation develops character in your players depends as much on you as it does on the sport itself. How can you build character in your players?

Having good character means modeling appropriate behaviors for sport and life. That means more than just saying the right things. What you say and what you do must match. There is no place in coaching for the "Do as I say, not as I do" philosophy. Challenge, support, encourage, and reward every youngster, and your players will be more likely to accept, even celebrate, their differences. Be in control before, during, and after all practices and contests. And don't be afraid to admit that you were wrong. No one is perfect!

Consider the following steps to being a good role model:

◎ Take stock of your strengths and weaknesses.

◎ Build on your strengths.

◎ Set goals for yourself to improve upon those areas you would not like to see copied.

◎ If you slip up, apologize to your team and to yourself. You'll do better next time.

Humor

Humor is an often-overlooked coaching tool. For our use it means having the ability to laugh at yourself and with your players during practices and contests. Nothing helps balance the tone of a serious skill-learning session like a chuckle or two. And a sense of humor puts in perspective the many mistakes your players will make. So don't get upset over each miscue or respond negatively to erring players. Allow your players and yourself to enjoy the ups, and don't dwell on the downs.

Here are some tips for injecting humor into your practices:

◎ Make practices fun by including a variety of activities.

◎ Keep all players involved in games and skill practices.

◎ Consider laughter by your players a sign of enjoyment, not of waning discipline.

◎ Smile!

Communicating As a Coach

In chapter 1 you learned about the tools needed to COACH: Comprehension, Outlook, Affection, Character, and Humor. These are essentials for effective coaching; without them, you'd have a difficult time getting started. But none of the tools will work if you don't know how to use them with your athletes—and this requires skillful communication. This chapter examines what communication is and how you can become a more effective communicator-coach.

What's Involved in Communication?

Coaches often mistakenly believe that communication involves only instructing players to do something, but verbal commands are only a small part of the communication process. More than half of what is communicated is nonverbal. So remember when you are coaching: Actions speak louder than words.

Communication in its simplest form involves two people: a sender and a receiver. The sender transmits the message verbally, through facial expressions, and possibly through body language. Once the message is sent, the receiver must assimilate it successfully. A receiver who fails to attend or listen will miss parts, if not all, of the message.

How Can I Send More Effective Messages?

Young athletes often have little understanding of the rules and skills of basketball and probably even less confidence in playing it. So they need accurate, understandable, and supportive messages to help them along. That's why your verbal and nonverbal messages are so important.

Verbal Messages

"Sticks and stones may break my bones, but words will never hurt me" isn't true. Spoken words can have a strong and long-lasting effect. And coaches' words are particularly influential because youngsters place great importance on what coaches say. Perhaps you, like many former youth sport participants, have a difficult time remembering much of anything you were told by your elementary school teachers, but you can still recall several specific things your coaches at that level said to you. Such is the lasting effect of a coach's comments to a player.

Whether you are correcting misbehavior, teaching a player how to pass the ball, or praising a player for good effort, you should consider a number of things when sending a message verbally. They include the following:

- Be positive and honest.
- State it clearly and simply.
- Say it loud enough, and say it again.
- Be consistent.

Be Positive and Honest

Nothing turns people off like hearing someone nag all the time, and athletes react similarly to a coach who gripes constantly. Kids particularly need encouragement because they often doubt their ability to perform in a sport. So look for and tell your players what they did well.

But don't cover up poor or incorrect play with rosy words of praise. Kids know all too well when they've erred, and no cheerfully expressed cliche can undo their mistakes. If you fail to acknowledge players' errors, your athletes will think you are a phony.

A good way to correct a performance error is to first point out what the athlete did correctly. Then explain in a positive way what he or she is doing wrong and show him or her how to correct it. Finish by encouraging the athlete and emphasizing the correct performance.

Be sure not to follow a positive statement with the word *but*. For example, don't say, "That was good location on your pass, Kelly. But if you follow through a little more, you'll get a little more zip on the ball." Saying it this way causes many kids to ignore the positive statement and focus on the negative one. Instead, say something like, "That was good location on your pass, Kelly. And if you follow through a little more, you'll get a little more zip on the ball. That was right on target. That's the way to go."

State It Clearly and Simply

Positive and honest messages are good, but only if expressed directly in words your players understand. "Beating around the bush" is ineffective and inefficient. And if you do ramble, your players will miss the point of your message and probably lose interest. Here are some tips for saying things clearly:

- Organize your thoughts before speaking to your athletes.
- Explain things thoroughly, but don't bore them with long-winded monologues.
- Use language your players can understand. However, avoid trying to be hip by using their age group's slang vocabulary.

Say It Loud Enough, and Say It Again

Talk to your team in a voice that all members can hear and interpret. A crisp, vigorous voice commands attention and respect; garbled and weak speech is tuned out. It's OK, in fact, appropriate, to soften your voice when speaking to a player individually about a personal problem. But most of the time your messages will be for all your players to hear, so make sure they can! An enthusiastic voice also motivates players and tells them you enjoy being their coach. A word of caution, however: Don't dominate the setting with a booming voice that distracts attention from players' performances.

Sometimes what you say, even if stated loudly and clearly, won't sink in the first time. This may be particularly true when young athletes hear words they don't understand. To avoid boring repetition and yet still get your message across, say the same thing in a slightly different way. For instance, you might first tell your players, "Play tighter defense!" If they don't appear to understand, you might say, "When your opponent is one pass away from the ball, you need to cut off the passing lane." The second form of the message may get through to players who missed it the first time around.

Be Consistent

People often say things in ways that imply a different message. For example, a touch of sarcasm added to the words "Way to go!" sends an entirely different message than the words themselves suggest. Avoid sending such mixed messages. Keep the tone of your voice consistent with the words you use. And don't say something one day and contradict it the next; players will get their wires crossed.

Nonverbal Messages

Just as you should be consistent in the tone of voice and words you use, you should also keep your verbal and nonverbal messages consistent. An extreme example of failing to do this would be shaking your head, indicating disapproval, while at the same time telling a player "Nice try." Which is the player to believe, your gesture or your words?

Messages can be sent nonverbally in a number of ways. Facial expressions and body language are just two of the more obvious forms of nonverbal signals that can help you when you coach.

Facial Expressions

The look on a person's face is the quickest clue to what he or she thinks or feels. Your players know this, so they will study your face, looking for any sign that will tell them more than the words you say. Don't try to fool them by putting on a happy or blank "mask." They'll see through it, and you'll lose credibility.

Serious, stone-faced expressions are no help to kids who need cues as to how they are performing. They will just assume you're unhappy or disinterested. Don't be afraid to smile. A smile from a coach can give a great boost to an unsure athlete. Plus, a smile lets your players know that you are happy coaching them. But don't overdo it, or your players won't be able to tell when you are genuinely pleased by something they've done or when you are just putting on a smiling face.

Body Language

What would your players think you were feeling if you came to practice slouched over, with your head down and shoulders slumped? Tired? Bored? Unhappy? What would they think you were feeling if you watched them during a contest with your hands on your hips, your jaws clenched, and your face reddened? Upset with them? Disgusted with a referee? Mad at a fan? Probably some or all of these things would enter your players' minds. And none of these impressions is the kind you want your players to have of you. That's why you should carry yourself in a pleasant, confident, and vigorous manner. Such a posture not only projects happiness with your coaching role but also provides a good example for your young players, who may model your behavior.

Physical contact can also be a very important use of body language. A handshake, a pat on the head, an arm around the shoulder, or even a big hug are effective ways of showing approval, concern, affection, and joy to your players. Youngsters are especially in need of this type of nonverbal message. Keep within the obvious moral and legal limits, of course, but don't be reluctant to touch your players, sending a message that can only truly be expressed in that way.

How Can I Improve My Receiving Skills?

Now, let's examine the other half of the communication process—receiving messages. Too often very good senders are very poor receivers of messages. But as a coach of young athletes, you must be able to fulfill both roles effectively.

The requirements for receiving messages are quite simple, but receiving skills are perhaps less satisfying and therefore underdeveloped compared to sending skills. People seem to naturally enjoy hearing themselves talk more than hearing others talk. But if you read about the keys to receiving messages and make a strong effort to use them with your players, you'll be surprised by what you've been missing.

Attention!

First, you must pay attention; you must want to hear what others have to communicate to you. That's not always easy when you're busy coaching and have many things competing for your attention. But in one-on-one or team meetings with players, you must really focus on what they are telling you, both verbally and nonverbally. You'll be amazed at the little signals you pick up. Not only will such focused attention help you catch every word your players say, but also you'll notice your players' moods and physical states. In addition, you'll get an idea of your players' feelings toward you and other players on the team.

Listen CARE-FULLY

How we receive messages from others, perhaps more than anything else we do, demonstrates how much we care for the sender and what that person has to tell us. If you care little for your players or have little regard for what they have to say, it will show in how you attend and listen to them. Check yourself. Do you find your mind wandering to what you are going to do after practice while one of your players is talking to you? Do you frequently have to ask your players, "What did you say?" If so, you need to work on your receiving mechanics of attending and listening. But perhaps the most critical question you should ask yourself, if you find that you're missing the messages your players send, is this: Do I care?

Providing Feedback

So far we've discussed separately the sending and receiving of messages. But we all know that senders and receivers switch roles several times during an interaction. One person initiates a communication by sending a message to another person, who then receives the message. The receiver then switches roles and becomes the sender by responding to the person who sent the initial message. These verbal and nonverbal responses are called *feedback*.

Your players will be looking to you for feedback all the time. They will want to know how you think they are performing, what you think of their ideas, and whether their efforts please you. Obviously, you can respond in many different ways. How you respond will strongly affect your players. They will respond most favorably to positive feedback.

Praising players when they have performed or behaved well is an effective way of getting them to repeat (or try to repeat) that behavior in the future. And positive feedback for effort is an especially effective way to motivate youngsters to work on difficult skills. So rather than shouting and providing negative feedback to players who have made mistakes, try offering players positive feedback, letting them know what they did correctly and how they can improve.

Sometimes just the way you word feedback can make it more positive than negative. For example, instead of saying, "Don't shoot the ball that way," you might say, "Shoot the ball this way." Then your players will be focusing on what to do instead of what not to do.

You can give positive feedback verbally and nonverbally. Telling a player, especially in front of teammates, that he or she has performed well, is a great way to boost the confidence of a youngster. And a pat on the back or a handshake can be a very tangible way of communicating your recognition of a player's performance.

Who Else Do I Need to Communicate With?

Coaching involves not only sending and receiving messages and providing proper feedback to players, but also interacting with parents, fans, game referees, and opposing coaches. If you don't communicate effectively with these groups of people, your coaching career will be unpleasant and short-lived. So try the following suggestions for communicating with these groups.

Parents

A player's parents need to be assured that their son or daughter is under the direction of a coach who is both knowledgeable about the sport and concerned about the youngster's well-being. You can put their worries to rest by holding a preseason parent-orientation meeting in which you describe your background and your approach to coaching.

If parents contact you with a concern during the season, listen to them closely and try to offer positive responses. If you need to communicate with parents, catch them after a practice, give them a phone call, or send a note through the mail. Messages sent to parents through players are too often lost, misinterpreted, or forgotten.

Fans

The stands probably won't be overflowing at your contests, but that only means that you'll more easily hear the few fans who criticize your coaching. When you hear something negative said about the job you're doing, don't respond. Keep calm, consider whether the message had any value, and if not, forget it. Acknowledging critical, unwarranted comments from a fan during a contest will only encourage others to voice their opinions. So put away your "rabbit ears" and communicate to fans, through your actions, that you are a confident, competent coach.

Prepare your players for fans' criticisms. Tell them it is you, not the spectators, they should listen to. If you notice that one of your players is rattled by a fan's comment, reassure the player that your evaluation is more objective and favorable—and the one that counts.

Contest Referees

How you communicate with referees will have a great influence on the way your players behave toward them. Therefore, you need to set an example. Greet referees with a handshake, an introduction, and perhaps some casual conversation about the upcoming contest. Indicate your respect for them before, during, and after the contest. Don't make nasty remarks, shout, or use disrespectful body gestures. Your players will see you do it, and they'll get the idea that such behavior is appropriate. Plus, if the referee hears or sees you, the communication between the two of you will break down.

Opposing Coaches

Make an effort to visit with the coach of the opposing team before the game. During the game, don't get into a personal feud with the opposing coach. Remember, it's the kids, not the coaches, who are competing. And by getting along well with the opposing coach, you'll show your players that competition involves cooperation.

chapter 3

Providing for Players' Safety

One of your players appears to break free downcourt, dribbling the ball toward the basket for an apparent layup. Out of nowhere races a defender who catches up with and accidentally undercuts your player. You see that your player is not getting up and seems to be in pain. What do you do?

No coach wants to see players get hurt. But injury remains a reality of sport participation; consequently, you must be prepared to provide first aid when injuries occur and to protect yourself against unjustified lawsuits. Fortunately, there are many preventive measures coaches can institute to reduce the risk. In this chapter we describe steps you can take to prevent injuries, first aid and emergency responses for when injuries occur, and your legal responsibilities as a coach.

The Game Plan for Safety

You can't prevent all injuries from happening, but you can take preventive measures that give your players the best possible chance for injury-free participation. In creating the safest possible environment for your athletes, we'll explore what you can do in these six areas:

1. Preseason physical examinations
2. Physical conditioning
3. Equipment and facilities inspection
4. Matching athletes and inherent risks
5. Proper supervision and record keeping
6. Environmental conditions

We'll begin with what should take place *before* the season begins: the preseason physical examination.

Preseason Physical Examination

We recommend that your players have a physical examination before participating in basketball. The exam should address the most likely areas of medical concern and identify youngsters at high risk. We also suggest that you have players' parents or guardians sign a participation agreement form and a release form to allow their children to be treated in case of an emergency.

Physical Conditioning

Players need to be in, or get in, shape to play the game at the level expected. To do so, they'll need to have adequate *cardiorespiratory fitness* and *muscular fitness.*

Cardiorespiratory fitness involves the body's ability to store and use oxygen and fuels efficiently to power muscle contractions. As players get in better shape, their bodies are able to more efficiently deliver oxygen and fuels to muscles and carry off carbon dioxides and other wastes. Basketball involves lots of running; most players will have to be able to move almost continuously and make short bursts throughout a game.

Youngsters who aren't as fit as their peers often overextend in trying to make up for their lack of fitness, which could result in lightheadedness and nausea.

An advantage of teaching basketball with the games approach is that kids are active during almost the entire practice; there is no standing around in lines, watching teammates take part in drills. Players will be attaining higher levels of cardiorespiratory fitness as the season progresses simply by taking part in practice. However, watch closely for signs of low levels of cardiorespiratory fitness; don't let your athletes do too much until they're fit. You might privately counsel youngsters who appear overly winded, suggesting that they train outside of practice to increase their fitness.

Muscular fitness encompasses strength, muscle endurance, power, speed, and flexibility. This type of fitness is affected by physical maturity, as well as strength training and other types of training. Your players will likely exhibit a relatively wide range of muscular fitness. Those who have greater muscular fitness will be able to run faster and pass farther. They will also sustain fewer muscular injuries, and any injuries that do occur will tend to be more minor in nature. And in case of injury, recovery rate is accelerated in those with higher levels of muscular fitness.

Two other components of fitness and injury prevention are the warm-up and the cool-down. Although young bodies are generally very limber, they too, can get tight from inactivity. The warm-up should address each muscle group and get the heart rate elevated in preparation for strenuous activity. Have players warm up for 5 to 10 minutes by playing easy games and stretching.

As practice winds down, slow players' heart rates with an easy jog or walk. Then have players stretch for 5 minutes to help avoid stiff muscles and make them less tight before the next practice or contest.

Equipment and Facilities Inspection

Another way to prevent injuries is to examine regularly the court on which your players practice and play. Remove hazards, report conditions you cannot remedy, and request maintenance as necessary. If unsafe conditions exist, either make adaptations to avoid risk to your players' safety or stop the practice or game until safe conditions have been restored.

Player Match-Ups and Inherent Risks

We recommend you group teams in two-year age ranges if possible. You'll encounter fewer mismatches in physical maturation with narrow age ranges. Even so, two 12-year-old boys might differ by 90 pounds in weight, a foot in height, and three or four years in emotional and intellectual maturity. This presents dangers for the less mature. Whenever possible, match players against opponents of similar size and physical maturity. Such an approach gives smaller, less mature youngsters a better chance to succeed and avoid injury while providing more mature players with a greater challenge. Closely supervise games so that the more mature do not put the less mature at undue risk.

Proper matching helps protect you from certain liability concerns. But you must also warn players of the inherent risks involved in playing basketball, because "failure to warn" is one of the most successful arguments in lawsuits against coaches. So, thoroughly explain the inherent risks of basketball, and make sure each player knows, understands, and appreciates those risks.

The preseason parent-orientation meeting is a good opportunity to explain the risks of the sport to both parents and players. It is also a good occasion on which to have both the players and their parents sign waivers releasing you from liability should an injury occur. Such waivers do not relieve you of responsibility for your players' well-being, but they are recommended by lawyers.

Proper Supervision and Record Keeping

To ensure players' safety, you will need to provide both general supervision and specific supervision. *General supervision* is being in the area of activity so that you can see and hear what is happening. You should be

- immediately accessible to the activity and able to oversee the entire activity,
- alert to conditions that may be dangerous to players and ready to take action to protect them, and
- able to react immediately and appropriately to emergencies.

Specific supervision is direct supervision of an activity at practice. For example, you should provide specific supervision when you teach new skills and continue it until your athletes understand the requirements of the activity, the risks involved, and their own ability to perform in light of these risks. You need to also provide specific supervision when you notice either players breaking rules or a change in the condition of your athletes.

As a general rule, the more dangerous the activity, the more specific the supervision required. This suggests that more specific supervision is required with younger and less experienced athletes.

As part of your supervision duty, you are expected to foresee potentially dangerous situations and to be positioned to help prevent them from occurring. This requires that you know basketball well, especially the rules that are intended to provide for safety. Prohibit dangerous horseplay, and hold practices only under safe weather conditions (e.g., cancel practice if severe winter weather is forecast). These specific supervisory activities, applied consistently, will make the play environment safer for your players and will help protect you from liability if a mishap does occur.

For further protection, keep records of your season plans, practice plans, and players' injuries. Season and practice plans come in handy when you need evidence that players have been taught certain skills, whereas accurate, detailed injury-report forms offer protection against unfounded lawsuits. Ask for these forms from your sponsoring organization (appendix A has a sample injury-report form), and hold onto these records for several years so that an "old basketball injury" of a former player doesn't come back to haunt you.

Environmental Conditions

Most problems due to environmental factors are related to excessive heat, though you should also consider other environmental factors such as severe weather and pollution. While the risks here for an indoor sport are relatively minimal, a little thought about the potential problems and a little effort to ensure adequate protection for your athletes will prevent most serious emergencies that are related to environmental conditions.

Heat

On hot, humid days the body has difficulty cooling itself. Because the air is already saturated with water vapor (humidity), sweat doesn't evaporate as easily. Therefore, body sweat is a less effective cooling agent, and the body retains extra heat. Hot, humid environments make athletes prone to heat exhaustion and heatstroke (see more on these in "Serious Injuries" on page 29). And if *you* think it's hot or humid, it's worse on the kids—not only because they're more active, but also because youngsters under the age of 12 have a more difficult time than adults regulating their body temperature. To provide for players' safety in hot or humid conditions, take the following preventive measures.

⊙ **Monitor weather conditions and adjust practices accordingly.** Figure 3.1 (page 22) shows the specific air temperatures and humidity percentages that can be hazardous.

⊙ **Acclimatize players to exercising in high heat and humidity.** Athletes can make adjustments to high heat and humidity over 7 to 10 days. During this time, hold practices at low to moderate activity levels and give the players water breaks every 20 minutes.

⊙ **Switch to light clothing.** Players should wear shorts and white T-shirts.

⊙ **Identify and monitor players who are prone to heat illness.** Players who are overweight, heavily muscled, or out of shape will be more prone to heat illness, as are athletes who work excessively hard or who have suffered heat illness before. Closely monitor these athletes and give them water breaks every 15 to 20 minutes.

⊙ **Make sure athletes replace water lost through sweat.** Encourage your players to drink one liter of water each day outside of practice and contest times, to drink eight ounces of water every 20 minutes during practice or competition, and to drink four to eight ounces of water 20 minutes before practice or competition.

⊙ **Replenish electrolytes lost through sweat.** Sodium (salt) and potassium are lost through sweat. The best way to replace these nutrients is by eating a normal diet that contains fresh fruits and vegetables. Bananas are a good source of potassium. The normal American diet contains plenty of salt, so players don't need to go overboard in salting their food to replace lost sodium.

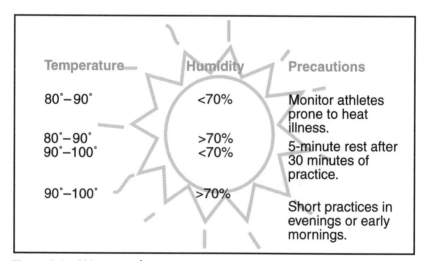

Temperature	Humidity	Precautions
80°–90°	<70%	Monitor athletes prone to heat illness.
80°–90°	>70%	
90°–100°	<70%	5-minute rest after 30 minutes of practice.
90°–100°	>70%	Short practices in evenings or early mornings.

Figure 3.1   Warm-weather precautions.

Water, Water Everywhere

Encourage players to drink plenty of water before, during, and after practice. Because water makes up 45 percent to 65 percent of a youngster's body weight and water weighs about a pound per pint, the loss of even a little bit of water can have severe consequences for the body's systems. And it doesn't have to be hot and humid for players to become dehydrated. Nor do players have to feel thirsty; in fact, by the time they are aware of their thirst, they are long overdue for a drink.

Severe Weather

Severe weather refers to a host of potential dangers, including lightning storms and tornadoes. Sometimes basketball practices might be held outside; if you do practice outdoors, you'll need to pay heed to this information.

Lightning is of special concern because it can come up quickly and can cause great harm or even kill. For each 5-second count from the flash of lightning to the bang of thunder, lightning is one mile away. A flash-bang of 10 seconds means lightning is two miles away; a flash-bang of 15 seconds indicates lightning is three miles away. A practice or competition should be stopped for the day if lightning is three miles away or less (15 seconds or less from flash to bang).

Safe places in which to take cover when lightning strikes are fully enclosed metal vehicles with the windows up, enclosed buildings, and low ground (under cover of bushes, if possible). It's *not* safe to be near metallic objects—flag poles, fences, light poles, metal bleachers, and so on. Also avoid trees, water, and open fields.

Cancel practice when under either a tornado watch or warning. If for some reason you are practicing or competing when a tornado is nearby, you should get inside a building if possible. If not, lie in a ditch or other low-lying area or crouch near a strong building, and use your arms to protect your head and neck.

The keys to handling severe weather are caution and prudence. Don't try to get that last 10 minutes of practice in if lightning is on the horizon. Don't continue to play in heavy rains. Many storms can strike both quickly and ferociously. Respect the weather and play it safe.

Air Pollution

Poor air quality and smog can present real dangers to your players, even playing indoors. Both short- and long-term lung damage are possible from participating in unsafe air. While it's true that participating in clean air is not possible in many areas, restricting activity is recommended when the air-quality ratings are worse than moderate or when there is a smog alert. Your local health department or air-quality control board can inform you of the air-quality ratings for your area and when restricting activities is recommended.

Responding to Players' Injuries

No matter how good and thorough your prevention program is, injuries may occur. When injury does strike, chances are you will be the one in charge. The severity and nature of the injury will determine how actively involved you'll be in treating the injury. But regardless of how seriously a player is hurt, it is your responsibility to know what steps to take. So let's look at how you should prepare to provide basic emergency care to your injured athletes and take the appropriate action when an injury does occur.

Being Prepared

Being prepared to provide basic emergency care involves three steps: being trained in cardiopulmonary resuscitation (CPR) and first aid, having an appropriately stocked first-aid kit on hand at practices and games, and having an emergency plan.

CPR and First-Aid Training

We recommend that all coaches receive CPR and first-aid training from a nationally recognized organization (the National Safety Council, the American Heart Association, the American Red Cross, or the American Sport Education Program). You should be certified based on a practical test and a written test of knowledge. CPR training should include pediatric and adult basic life support and obstructed airway procedures.

First-Aid Kit

A well-stocked first-aid kit should include the following:

- List of emergency phone numbers
- Change for a pay phone

- Face shield (for rescue breathing and CPR)
- Bandage scissors
- Plastic bags for crushed ice
- 3-inch and 4-inch elastic wraps
- Triangular bandages
- Sterile gauze pads—3-inch and 4-inch squares
- Saline solution for eyes
- Contact lens case
- Mirror
- Penlight
- Tongue depressors
- Cotton swabs
- Butterfly strips
- Bandage strips—assorted sizes
- Alcohol or peroxide
- Antibacterial soap
- First aid cream or antibacterial ointment
- Petroleum jelly
- Tape adherent and tape remover
- 1-½-inch white athletic tape
- Prewrap
- Sterile gauze rolls
- Insect sting kit
- Safety pins
- ⅛-inch, ¼-inch, and ½-inch foam rubber
- Disposable surgical gloves
- Thermometer

Emergency Plan

An emergency plan is the final step in preparing to take appropriate action for severe or serious injuries. The plan calls for three steps:

1. **Evaluate the injured player.** Your CPR and first-aid training will guide you here.

2. **Call the appropriate medical personnel.** If possible, delegate the responsibility of seeking medical help to another calm and responsible adult who is on hand for all practices and games. Write out a list of emergency phone numbers and keep it with you at practices and games. Include the following phone numbers:

○ Rescue unit
○ Hospital
○ Physician
○ Police
○ Fire department

Take each athlete's emergency information to every practice and game (see appendix B). This information includes the person to contact in case of an emergency, what types of medications the athlete is using, what types of drugs he or she is allergic to, and so on.

Give an emergency response card (see appendix C) to the contact person calling for emergency assistance. This provides the information the contact person needs to convey and will help keep the person calm, knowing that everything he or she needs to communicate is on the card. Also complete an injury report form (see appendix A) and keep it on file for any injury that occurs.

3. **Provide first aid.** If medical personnel are not on hand at the time of the injury, you should provide first aid care to the extent of your qualifications. Again, while your CPR and first aid training will guide you here, the following are important guidelines:

Do not move the injured athlete if the injury is to the head, neck, or back; if a large joint (ankle, knee, elbow, shoulder) is dislocated; or if the pelvis, a rib, or an arm or leg is fractured.

○ Calm the injured athlete and keep others away from him or her as much as possible.
○ Evaluate whether the athlete's breathing is stopped or irregular, and if necessary, clear the airway with your fingers.
○ Administer artificial respiration if the athlete's breathing has stopped. Administer CPR if the athlete's circulation has stopped.
○ Remain with the athlete until medical personnel arrive.

Emergency Steps

Your emergency plan should follow this sequence:

1. Check the athlete's level of consciousness.

2. Send a contact person to call the appropriate medical personnel and to call the athlete's parents.

3. Send someone to wait for the rescue team and direct them to the injured athlete.

4. Assess the injury.

5. Administer first aid.

6. Assist emergency medical personnel in preparing the athlete for transportation to a medical facility.

7. Appoint someone to go with the athlete if the parents are not available. This person should be responsible, calm, and familiar with the athlete. Assistant coaches or parents are best for this job.

8. Complete an injury report form while the incident is fresh in your mind (see appendix A).

Taking Appropriate Action

Proper CPR and first-aid training, a well-stocked first-aid kit, and an emergency plan help prepare you to take appropriate action when an injury occurs. We spoke in the previous section about the importance of providing first aid *to the extent of your qualifications*. Don't "play doctor" with injuries; sort out minor injuries that you can treat from those for which you need to call for medical assistance.

Next we'll look at taking the appropriate action for minor injuries and more serious injuries.

Minor Injuries

Although no injury seems minor to the person experiencing it, most injuries are neither life-threatening nor severe enough to restrict participation. When such injuries occur, you can take an active role in their initial treatment.

Scrapes and Cuts. When one of your players has an open wound, the first thing you should do is put on a pair of disposable surgical gloves or some other effective blood barrier. Then follow these four steps:

1. *Stop the bleeding* by applying direct pressure with a clean dressing to the wound and elevating it. The player may be able to apply this pressure while you put on your gloves. Do not remove the dressing if it becomes soaked with blood. Instead, place an additional dressing on top of the one already in place. If bleeding continues, elevate the injured area above the heart and maintain pressure.

2. *Cleanse the wound* thoroughly once the bleeding is controlled. A good rinsing with a forceful stream of water, and perhaps light scrubbing with soap, will help prevent infection.

3. *Protect the wound* with sterile gauze or a bandage strip. If the player continues to participate, apply protective padding over the injured area.

4. *Remove and dispose of gloves* carefully to prevent you or anyone else from coming into contact with blood.

For bloody noses not associated with serious facial injury, have the athlete sit and lean slightly forward. Then pinch the player's nostrils shut. If the bleeding continues after several minutes, or if the athlete has a history of nosebleeds, seek medical assistance.

Treating Bloody Injuries

You shouldn't let a fear of acquired immune deficiency syndrome (AIDS) stop you from helping a player. You are only at risk if you allow contaminated blood to come in contact with an open wound, so the surgical disposable gloves that you wear will protect you from AIDS should one of your players carry this disease. Check with your director or your organization for more information about protecting yourself and your participants from AIDS.

Strains and Sprains. The physical demands of basketball practices and games often result in injury to the muscles or tendons (strains) or to the ligaments (sprains). When your players suffer minor strains or sprains, immediately apply the PRICE method of injury care:

P – Protect the athlete and injured body part from further danger or trauma.

R – Rest the area to avoid further damage and foster healing.

I – Ice the area to reduce swelling and pain.

C – Compress the area by securing an ice bag in place with an elastic wrap.

E – Elevate the injury above heart level to keep the blood from pooling in the area.

Bumps and Bruises. Inevitably, basketball players make contact with each other and with the ground. If the force applied to a body part at impact is great enough, a bump or bruise will result. Many players continue playing with such sore spots, but if the bump or bruise is large and painful, you should act appropriately. Use the PRICE method for injury care and monitor the injury. If swelling, discoloration, and pain have lessened, the player may resume participation with protective padding; if not, the player should be examined by a physician.

Serious Injuries

Head, neck, and back injuries; fractures; and injuries that cause a player to lose consciousness are among a class of injuries that you cannot and should not try to treat yourself. In these cases you should follow the emergency plan outlined on page 27. We do want to examine more closely your role, however, in preventing and handling two heat illnesses: heat exhaustion and heatstroke.

Heat Exhaustion. Heat exhaustion is a shock-like condition caused by dehydration and electrolyte depletion. Symptoms include headache, nausea, dizziness, chills, fatigue, and extreme thirst. Profuse sweating is a key sign of heat exhaustion. Other signs include pale, cool, and clammy skin; rapid, weak pulse; loss of coordination; and dilated pupils.

A player suffering from heat exhaustion should rest in a cool, shaded area; drink cool water; and have ice applied to the neck, back, or abdomen to help cool the body. You may have to administer CPR if necessary or send for emergency medical assistance if the athlete doesn't recover or his or her condition worsens. Under no conditions should the athlete return to activity that day or before he or she regains all the weight lost through sweat. If the player had to see a physician, he or she shouldn't return to the team until he or she has a written release from the physician.

Heatstroke. Heatstroke is a life-threatening condition in which the body stops sweating and body temperature rises dangerously high. It occurs when dehydration causes a malfunction in the body's temperature control center in the brain. Symptoms include the feeling of being on fire (extremely hot), nausea, confusion, irritability, and fatigue. Signs include hot, dry, and flushed or red skin (this is a key sign); lack of sweat; rapid pulse; rapid breathing; constricted pupils; vomiting; diarrhea; and possibly seizures, unconsciousness, or respiratory or cardiac arrest. See figure 3.2 (page 30) for heat exhaustion and heatstroke symptoms.

Send for emergency medical assistance immediately and have the player rest in a cool, shaded area. Remove excess clothing and equipment from the player, and cool the player's body with cool, wet towels or by pouring cool water over him or her. Apply ice packs to the armpits, neck, back, abdomen, and between the legs. If the player is conscious, have

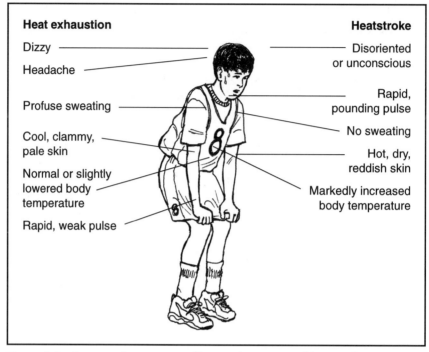

Heat exhaustion

Dizzy

Headache

Profuse sweating

Cool, clammy, pale skin

Normal or slightly lowered body temperature

Rapid, weak pulse

Heatstroke

Disoriented or unconscious

Rapid, pounding pulse

No sweating

Hot, dry, reddish skin

Markedly increased body temperature

Figure 3.2 Signs and symptoms of heat exhaustion and heatstroke.

him or her drink cool water. If the player is unconscious, place the player on his or her side to allow fluids and vomit to drain from the mouth. An athlete who has suffered heatstroke may not return to the team until he or she has a written release from a physician.

Protecting Yourself

When one of your players is injured, naturally your first concern is his or her well-being. Your feelings for youngsters, after all, are what made you decide to coach. Unfortunately, there is something else that you must consider: Can you be held liable for the injury?

From a legal standpoint, a coach has nine duties to fulfill. We've discussed all but planning in this chapter; we'll explore planning in chapter 9. The following is a summary of your legal duties:

1. Provide a safe environment.
2. Properly plan the activity.
3. Provide adequate and proper equipment.

4. Match, or equate, athletes.

5. Warn of inherent risks in the sport.

6. Supervise the activity closely.

7. Evaluate athletes for injury or incapacitation.

8. Know emergency procedures and first aid.

9. Keep adequate records.

Keep records of your season plan and practice plans and of players' injuries. Season and practice plans come in handy when you need evidence that players have been taught certain skills, and injury reports offer protection against unfounded lawsuits. Hold onto these records for several years so that an "old injury" of a former player doesn't come back to haunt you.

In addition to fulfilling these nine legal duties, you should check your organization's insurance coverage and your insurance coverage to make sure these policies will protect you from liability.

chapter 4

The Games Approach to Coaching Basketball

Do you remember how as a kid you were taught by adults to play a sport, either in an organized sport program or physical education class? They probably taught you the basic skills using a series of drills that, if the truth be known, you found very boring. As you began to learn the basic skills, they eventually taught you the tactics of the game, showing you when to use these skills in various game situations. Do you remember how impatient you became during what seemed to be endless instruction, and how much you just wanted to play? Well, forget this traditional approach to teaching sport.

Now can you recall learning a sport by playing with a group of your friends in the neighborhood? You didn't learn the basic skills first; no time for that. You began playing immediately. If you didn't know the basic things to do, your friends told you quickly during the game so they could keep playing. Try to remember, because we're going to ask you to use a very similar approach to teaching basketball to young people called the games approach, an approach we think knocks the socks off the traditional approach.

On the surface, it would seem to make sense to introduce basketball by first teaching the basic skills of the sport and then the tactics of the game, but we've discovered that this approach has disadvantages. First, it teaches the skills of the sport out of the context of the game. Kids may learn to pass, dribble, and shoot the ball, but they find it difficult to use these skills in the real game. This is because they do not yet understand the fundamental tactics of basketball and do not appreciate how best to use their new found skills.

Second, learning skills by doing drills outside of the context of the game is so-o-o-o boring. The single biggest turnoff about adults teaching kids sport is that we overorganize the instruction and deprive kids of their intrinsic desire to play the game.

As a coach we're asking that you teach basketball the games approach way. Clear the traditional approach out of your mind. Once you fully understand the games approach, you'll quickly see its superiority in teaching basketball. Not only will kids learn the game better, but you and your players will have much more fun. And as a bonus, you'll have far fewer discipline problems.

With the games approach to teaching basketball, we begin with a game. This will be a modified and much smaller game designed to suit the age and ability of the players. As the kids play in these "mini" games, you can begin to help them understand the nature of the game and to appreciate simple concepts of positioning and tactics. When your players understand what they must do in the game, they are then eager to develop the skills to play the game. Now that players are motivated to learn the skills, you can demonstrate the skills of the game, practice using game like drills, and provide individual instruction by identifying players' errors and helping to correct them.

In the traditional approach to teaching sports, players do this:

Learn the skill → **Learn the tactics** → **Play the game**

In the games approach players do this:

Play the game → **Learn the tactics** → **Learn the skill**

In the past we have placed too much emphasis on the learning of skills and not enough on learning how to play skillfully—that is, how to use those skills in competition. The games approach, in contrast, emphasizes learning what to do first, then how to do it. Moreover— and this is a really important point—the games approach lets kids discover what to do in the game not by you telling them, but by their experiencing it. What you do as an effective coach is help them discover what they've experienced.

In contrast to the "skill-drill-kill the enthusiasm" approach, the games approach is a guided discovery method of teaching. It empowers your kids to solve the problems that arise in the game, and that's a big part of the fun in learning a game.

Now let's look more closely at the games approach to see the four-step process for teaching basketball:

1. Play a modified basketball game.
2. Help the players discover what they need to do to play the game successfully.
3. Teach the skills of the game.
4. Practice the skills in another game.

Step 1. Play a Modified Basketball Game

Okay, it's the first day of practice; some of the kids are eager to get started, while others are obviously apprehensive. Some have rarely shot a ball, most don't know the rules, and none knows the positions in basketball. What do you do?

If you use the traditional approach, you start with a little warm-up activity, then line the players up for a simple shooting drill and go from there. With the games approach, you begin by playing a modified game that is developmentally appropriate for the level of the players and also designed to focus on learning a specific part of the game.

Modifying the game emphasizes a limited number of situations in the game. This is one way you "guide" your players to discover certain tactics in the game. For instance, you have your players play a 3 v 3 (three players versus three players) half-court game. The objective of the game is to make three passes before attempting to score. Playing the game this way forces players to think about what they have to do to keep possession of the ball.

Step 2. Help the Players Discover What They Need to Do

As your players are playing the game, look for the right spot to "freeze" the action, step in, and hold a brief question-and-answer session to discuss problems they were having in carrying out the goals of the game. You don't need to pop in on the first miscue, but if they repeat the same types of mental or physical mistakes a few times in a row, step in and ask them questions that relate to the aim of the game and the necessary skills required. The best time to interrupt the game is when you notice that they are having trouble carrying out the main goal, or aim, of the game. By freezing the action and asking questions, you'll help them understand

- what the aim of the game is,
- what they must do to achieve that aim, and
- what skills they must use to achieve that aim.

For example, if your players are playing a game in which the objective is to make three passes before attempting to score, but they are having trouble doing so, interrupt the action and ask them the following questions:

Coach: What are you supposed to do in this game?

Players: Pass the ball three times before scoring.

Coach: What does your team have to do to keep the ball for three passes in a row?

Players: Pass the ball.

Coach: Yes, and what else?

Players: You have to be able to get the pass, too.

Coach: OK. You have to be able to pass the ball and catch the ball when it's passed. Why don't we practice passing the ball and catching the pass?

Through the modified game and skillful questioning on your part, your players realize that accurate passing and catching skills are essential to their success in controlling the ball. Just as important, rather than *telling* them that passing and catching skills are critical, you led them to that discovery through a well-designed modified game and through questions. This questioning that leads to players' discovery is a crucial part of the games approach. Essentially you'll be asking your players—usually literally—"What do you need to do to succeed in this situation?"

Asking the right questions is a very important part of your teaching. At first asking questions will be difficult because your players have little or no experience with the game. And if you've learned sport through the traditional approach, you'll be tempted to tell your players how to play the game and not waste time asking them questions. Resist this powerful temptation to tell them what to do, and especially don't do so before they begin to play the game.

If your players have trouble understanding what to do, phrase your questions to let them choose between one option versus another. For example, if you ask them, "What's the fastest way to get the ball down the court?" and get answers such as "Throw it" or "Hit it," then ask, "Is it passing or dribbling?"

Immediately following the question-and-answer session you will begin a skill practice, which is Step 3 of the four-step process.

Sometimes players simply need to have more time playing the game, or you may need to modify the game further so that it is even easier for them to discover what they are to do. It'll take more patience on your part, but it's a powerful way to learn. Don't be reluctant to change the numbers in the teams or some aspect of the structure of the game to aid this discovery. In fact, we advocate playing "lopsided" games (3 v 1, 3 v 2) in the second game of each practice; we'll explain this concept in a moment.

Step 3. Teach the Skills of the Game

Only when your players recognize the skills they need to be successful in the game do you want to teach the specific skills through focused drills. This is when you use a more traditional approach to teaching sport skills, the "IDEA" approach, which we will describe in chapter 5.

Step 4. Practice the Skills in Another Game

Once the players have practiced the skill, you then put them in another game situation—this time a lopsided game (e.g., 3 v 1, 3 v 2). Why use lopsided teams? It's simple: As a coach, you want your players to experience success as they're learning skills. The best way to experience success early on is to create an advantage for the players. This makes it more likely that, for instance, in a 3 v 1 game, your three offensive players will be able to make three passes before attempting to score.

As players improve their skills you don't need to use lopsided games. At a certain point having a 3 v 1 or 4 v 2 advantage will be too easy for the kids and won't challenge them to hone their skills. At that point you lessen the advantage to, say, 3 v 2 or 4 v 3, or you may even decide that they're ready to practice the skill in even-sided competition. The key is to set up situations where your athletes experience success, yet are challenged in doing so. This will take careful monitoring on your part, but having kids play lopsided games as they are learning skills is a very effective way of helping them learn and improve.

And that's the games approach. Your players will get to *play* more in practice, and once they learn how the skills fit into their performance and enjoyment of the game, they'll be more motivated to work on those skills, which will help them to be successful.

Teaching and Shaping Skills

Coaching basketball is about teaching tactics, skills, fitness, values, and other useful things. It's also about "coaching" players before, during, and after contests. Teaching and coaching are closely related, but there are important differences. In this chapter we'll focus on principles of teaching, especially on teaching basketball skills. But many of the principles we'll discuss apply as well to teaching tactics, fitness concepts, and values.

Teaching Basketball Skills

Many people believe that the only qualification needed to teach a skill is to have performed it. It's helpful to have performed it, but there is much more than that to teaching successfully. And even if you haven't performed the skill before, you can still learn to teach successfully with the useful acronym IDEA:

I – Introduce the skill.

D – Demonstrate the skill.

E – Explain the skill.

A – Attend to players practicing the skill.

These are the basic steps of good teaching. Now we'll explain each step in greater detail.

Introduce the Skill

Players, especially young and inexperienced ones, need to know what skill they are learning and why they are learning it. You should therefore take these three steps every time you introduce a skill to your players:

1. Get your players' attention.
2. Name the skill.
3. Explain the importance of the skill.

Get Your Players' Attention

Because youngsters are easily distracted, use some method to get their attention. Some coaches use interesting news items or stories. Others use jokes. And still others simply project enthusiasm to get their players to listen. Whatever method you use, speak slightly above the normal volume and look your players in the eye when you speak.

Also, position players so they can see and hear you. Arrange the players in two or three evenly spaced rows, facing you. (Make sure there's no distracting activity behind you.) Then ask if all of them can see you before you begin.

Name the Skill

Although you might mention other common names for the skill, decide which one you'll use and stick with it. This will help avoid confusion and enhance communication among your players.

Explain the Importance of the Skill

Although the importance of a skill may be apparent to you, your players may be less able to see how the skill will help them become better basketball players. Offer them a reason for learning the skill and describe how the skill relates to more advanced skills.

> *The most difficult aspect of coaching is this: Coaches must learn to let athletes learn. Sport skills should be taught so they have meaning to the child, not just meaning to the coach.*
>
> — Rainer Martens, founder of the American Sport Education Program

Demonstrate the Skill

The demonstration step is the most important part of teaching sport skills to players who may never have done anything closely resembling the skill. They need a picture, not just words. They need to see how the skill is performed.

If you are unable to perform the skill correctly, have an assistant coach, one of your players, or someone else more skilled perform the demonstration. These tips will help make your demonstrations more effective:

⊙ Use correct form.

⊙ Demonstrate the skill several times.

⊙ Slow down the action, if possible, during one or two performances so players can see every movement involved in the skill.

⊙ Perform the skill at different angles so your players can get a full perspective of it.

⊙ Demonstrate the skill with both the right and the left hands.

Explain the Skill

Players learn more effectively when they're given a brief explanation of the skill along with the demonstration. Use simple terms and, if possible, relate the skill to previously learned skills. Ask your players whether they understand your description. A good technique is to ask the team to repeat your explanation. Ask questions like "What are you going to do first?" and "Then what?" Watch for when players look confused or uncertain, and repeat your explanation and demonstration at those points. If possible, use different words so your players get a chance to try to understand the skill from a different perspective.

Complex skills often are better understood when they are explained in more manageable parts. For instance, if you want to teach your players how to perform the crossover dribble, you might take the following steps:

1. Show them a correct performance of the entire skill, and explain its function in basketball.
2. Break down the skill and point out its component parts to your players.
3. Have players perform each of the component skills you have already taught them, such as controlling the dribble at knee level, dribbling with the head up to see the rim, and protecting the ball with the body and the nondribbling hand.
4. After players have demonstrated their ability to perform the separate parts of the skill in sequence, reexplain the entire skill.
5. Have players practice the skill in gamelike conditions.

One caution: Young players have short attention spans, and a long demonstration or explanation of the skill will bore them. So spend no more than a few minutes altogether on the introduction, demonstration, and explanation phases. Then get the players active in a game that calls on them to perform the skill. The total IDEA should be completed in 10 minutes or less, followed by games in which players practice the skill.

Attend to Players Practicing the Skill

If the skill you selected was within your players' capabilities and you have done an effective job of introducing, demonstrating, and explaining it, your players should be ready to attempt the skill. Some players may need to be physically guided through the movements during their first few attempts. Walking unsure athletes through the skill in this way will help them gain confidence to perform the skill on their own.

Your teaching duties don't end when all your athletes have demonstrated that they understand how to perform the skill. In fact, a significant part of your teaching will involve observing closely the hit-and-miss trial performances of your players. In the next section we'll guide you in shaping players' skills, and then we'll help you learn how to detect and correct errors, using positive feedback. Keep in mind that your feedback will have a great influence on your players' motivation to practice and improve their performances.

Remember, too, that players need individual instruction. So set aside a time before, during, or after practice to give individual help.

Helping Players Improve Skills

After you have successfully taught your players the fundamentals of a skill, your focus will be on helping them improve that skill. Players will learn skills and improve upon them at different rates, so don't get too frustrated. Instead, help them improve by shaping their skills and detecting and correcting errors.

Shaping Players' Skills

One of your principal teaching duties is to reward positive behavior—in terms of successful skill execution—when you see it. A player makes a good pass in practice, and you immediately say, "That's the way to extend! Good followthrough!" This, plus a smile and a "thumbs-up" gesture, go a long way toward reinforcing that technique in that player.

However, sometimes you may have a long, dry spell before you have any correct technique to reinforce. It's difficult to reward players when they aren't executing skills correctly. How can you shape their skills if this is the case?

Shaping skills takes practice on your players' part and patience on your part. Expect your players to make errors. Telling the player who made the great pass that she did a good job doesn't ensure that she'll make that pass the next time. Seeing inconsistency in your players' techniques can be frustrating. It's even more challenging to stay positive when your athletes repeatedly perform a skill incorrectly or lack enthusiasm for learning. It can certainly be frustrating to see athletes who seemingly don't heed your advice and continue to make the same mistakes. And when the athletes don't seem to care, you may wonder why you should.

Please know that it is normal to get frustrated at times when teaching skills. Nevertheless, part of successful coaching is controlling this frustration. Instead of getting upset, use these six guidelines for shaping skills:

1. **Think small initially.** Reward the first signs of behavior that approximate what you want. Then reward closer and closer approximations of the desired behavior. In short, use your reward power to shape the behavior you seek.

2. **Break skills into small steps.** For instance, in learning to dribble, one of your players does well in keeping the ball close to his body, but he's bouncing the ball too high and not shielding it with his body and nondribbling hand. Reinforce the correct technique of keeping the ball

close, and teach him how to dribble at knee level. When he masters that, focus on getting him to shield the ball from defenders.

3. **Develop one component of a skill at a time.** Don't try to shape two components of a skill at once. For example, in rebounding, players must first block their opponents out, then go for the ball. They should focus first on blocking out by putting their back against their opponent's chest, spreading a wide base, putting the hands up, and then going on for the ball. Athletes who have problems mastering a skill often do so because they're trying to improve two or more components at once. Help these athletes to isolate a single component.

4. **As athletes become more proficient at a skill, reinforce them only occasionally and only for the best examples of the skill behavior.** By focusing only on the best examples, you will help them continue to improve once they've mastered the basics.

5. **When athletes are trying to master a new skill, temporarily relax your standards for how you reward them.** As they focus on the new skill or attempt to integrate it with other skills, the old well-learned skills may temporarily degenerate.

6. **If, however, a well-learned skill degenerates for long, you may need to restore it by going back to the basics.**

Coaches often have more skilled players provide feedback to teammates as they practice skills. This can be effective, but proceed with caution: You must tell the skilled players exactly what to look for when their teammates are performing the skills. You must also tell them the corrections for the common errors of that skill.

We've looked at how to guide your athletes as they learn skills. Now let's look at another critical teaching principle that you should employ as you're shaping skills: detecting and correcting errors.

Detecting and Correcting Errors

Good coaches recognize that athletes make two types of errors: learning errors and performance errors. *Learning errors* are ones that occur because athletes don't know how to perform a skill; that is, they have not yet developed the correct motor program in the brain to perform a particular skill. *Performance errors* are made not because athletes don't know how to do the skill, but because they made a mistake in executing what they do know. There is no easy way to know whether a player is making learning or performance errors. Part of the art of coaching is being able to sort out which type of error each mistake is.

The process of helping your athletes correct errors begins with your observing and evaluating their performances to determine if the mistakes are learning or performance errors. For performance errors, you need to look for the reasons that your athletes are not performing as well as they know how. If the mistakes are learning errors, then you need to help them learn the skill, which is the focus of this section.

There is no substitute for knowing skills well in correcting learning errors. The better you understand a skill—not only how it is done correctly but also what causes learning errors—the more helpful you will be in correcting mistakes.

One of the most common coaching mistakes is to provide inaccurate feedback and advice on how to correct errors. Don't rush into error correction; wrong feedback or poor advice will hurt the learning process more than no feedback or advice. If you are uncertain about the cause of the problem or how to correct it, continue to observe and analyze until you are more sure. As a rule, you should see the error repeated several times before attempting to correct it.

Correct One Error at a Time

Suppose Jill, one of your forwards, is having trouble with her shooting. She's doing some things well, but you notice that she's extending her arm on too flat a trajectory, resulting in too low an arc, and not squaring up to face the basket on all of her shots. What do you do?

First, decide which error to correct first, because athletes learn more effectively when they attempt to correct one error at a time. Determine whether one error is causing the other; if so, have the athlete correct that error first, because it may eliminate the other error. In Jill's case, however, neither error is causing the other. In such cases, athletes should correct the error that will bring the greatest improvement when remedied—for Jill, this probably means squaring up to the basket. Correcting one error often motivates athletes to correct other errors.

Use Positive Feedback to Correct Errors

The positive approach to correcting errors includes emphasizing what to do instead of what not to do. Use compliments, praise, rewards, and encouragement to correct errors. Acknowledge correct performance as well as efforts to improve. By using the positive approach, you can help your athletes feel good about themselves and promote a strong desire to achieve.

When you're working with one athlete at a time, the positive approach to correcting errors includes four steps:

1. Praise effort and correct performance.
2. Give simple and precise feedback to correct errors.
3. Make sure the athlete understands your feedback.
4. Provide an environment that motivates the athlete to improve.

Let's take a brief look at each step.

Step 1: Praise Effort and Correct Performance. Praise your athlete for trying to perform a skill correctly and for performing any parts of it correctly. Praise the athlete immediately after he or she performs the skill, if possible. Keep the praise simple: "Good try," "Way to hustle," "Good form," "Good extension," or "That's the way to follow through." You can also use nonverbal feedback, such as smiling, clapping your hands, or any facial or body expression that shows approval.

Make sure you're sincere with your praise. Don't indicate that an athlete's effort was good when it wasn't. Usually an athlete knows when he or she has made a sincere effort to perform the skill correctly and perceives undeserved praise for what it is—untruthful feedback to make him or her feel good. Likewise, don't indicate that a player's performance was correct when it wasn't.

Step 2: Give Simple and Precise Feedback. Don't burden a player with a long or detailed explanation of how to correct an error. Give just enough feedback so the player can correct one error at a time. Before giving feedback, recognize that some athletes will readily accept it immediately after the error; others will respond better if you slightly delay the correction.

For errors that are complicated to explain and difficult to correct, try the following:

⊙ Explain and demonstrate what the athlete should have done. Do not demonstrate what the athlete did wrong.

⊙ Explain the cause or causes of the error, if this isn't obvious.

⊙ Explain why you are recommending the correction you have selected, if it's not obvious.

Step 3: Make Sure the Athlete Understands Your Feedback. If the athlete doesn't understand your feedback, he or she won't be able to correct the error. Ask him or her to repeat the feedback and to explain and demonstrate how it will be used. If the athlete can't do this, be patient and present your feedback again. Then have the athlete repeat the feedback after you're finished.

Step 4: Provide an Environment That Motivates the Athlete to Improve.
Your players won't always be able to correct their errors immediately
even if they do understand your feedback. Encourage them to "hang
tough" and stick with it when corrections are difficult or they seem
discouraged. For more difficult corrections, remind them that it will
take time, and the improvement will happen only if they work at it.
Look to encourage players with low self-confidence. Saying something
like, "You were dribbling at a much better speed today; with practice,
you'll be able to keep the ball closer to you and shield it from defenders," can motivate a player to continue to refine his or her skills.

Some athletes need to be more motivated to improve. Others may be
very self-motivated and need little help from you in this area at all;
with them you can practically ignore Step 4 when correcting an error.
While motivation comes from within, look to provide an environment
of positive instruction and encouragement to help your athletes improve.

A final note on correcting errors: Team sports such as basketball provide unique challenges in this endeavor. How do you provide individual feedback in a group setting using a positive approach? Instead
of yelling across the court to correct an error (and embarrassing the
player), substitute for the player who erred. Then make the correction
on the sidelines. This type of feedback has three advantages:

- The player will be more receptive to the one-on-one feedback.
- The other players are still active, still practicing skills, and unable to
  hear your discussion.
- Because the rest of the team is still playing, you'll feel compelled to
  make your comments simple and concise—which, as we've said, is
  more helpful to the player.

This doesn't mean you can't use the team setting to give specific, positive feedback. You can do so to emphasize correct group and individual
performances. Use this team feedback approach *only* for positive state-
ments, though. Keep any negative feedback for individual discussions.

Developing Practice Plans

You will need to create practice plans for each season. Each practice
plan should contain the following sections:

- Purpose
- Equipment
- Plan

Purpose sections focus on what you want to teach your players during each practice; they outline your main theme for each practice. The purpose should be drawn from your season plan (see chapter 9). Equipment sections note what you'll need to have on hand for that practice. Plan sections outline what you will do during each practice session. Each consists of these elements:

⊙ Warm-Up
⊙ Game 1
⊙ Skill Practice
⊙ Game 2
⊙ Cool-down and Review

You'll begin each session with about five minutes of warm-up activities. Then you'll have your players play a modified basketball game (look in chapter 8 for suggested games and chapter 9 for their use in season plans). You'll look for your cue to interrupt that game—your cue being when players are having problems with carrying out the basic goal or aim of the game. At this point you'll "freeze" the action, keeping the players where they are, and ask brief questions about the tactical problems the players encountered and what skills they need to solve those problems. (Review chapter 4 for more on interrupting a game and holding a question-and-answer session.)

Then you'll teach the skill the players need to acquire to successfully execute the tactic. During Skill Practice you'll use the IDEA approach:

⊙ Introduce the skill
⊙ Demonstrate the skill
⊙ Explain the skill
⊙ Attend to players practicing the skill

Your introduction, demonstration, and explanation of a skill should take no more than two to three minutes; then you'll attend to players and provide teaching cues or further demonstration as necessary as they practice the skill.

After the Skill Practices, you will usually have the athletes play another game or two to let them use the skills they have just learned and to understand them in the context of a game. During Game and Skill Practices, emphasize the importance of every player on the court moving and being involved in every play, whether they will be directly touching the ball or not. No player on the court should be standing around.

The Plan section continues with a cool down and stretching. As your players stretch you'll wrap up the practice with a few summary comments and remind them of the next practice or game day.

The games in chapter 8 include suggestions to help you modify the games. These suggestions will help you keep practices fun and provide activities for players with varying skill levels.

Although practicing using the games approach should reduce the need for discipline, there will be times when you'll have to deal with players who are misbehaving in practice. In the next section we'll help you handle these situations.

Dealing With Misbehavior

Athletes will misbehave at times; it's only natural. Following are two ways you can respond to misbehavior: through extinction or discipline.

Extinction

Ignoring a misbehavior—neither rewarding nor disciplining it—is called *extinction*. This can be effective under certain circumstances. In some situations, disciplining young people's misbehavior only encourages them to act up further because of the recognition they get. Ignoring misbehavior teaches youngsters that it is not worth your attention.

Sometimes, though, you cannot wait for a behavior to fizzle out. When players cause danger to themselves or others or disrupt the activities of others, you need to take immediate action. Tell the offending player that the behavior must stop and that discipline will follow if it doesn't. If the athlete doesn't stop misbehaving after the warning, discipline.

Extinction also doesn't work well when a misbehavior is self-rewarding. For example, you may be able to keep from grimacing if a youngster kicks you in the shin, but he or she still knows you were hurt. Therein lies the reward. In these circumstances, it is also necessary to discipline the player for the undesirable behavior.

Extinction works best in situations in which players are seeking recognition through mischievous behaviors, clowning, or grandstanding. Usually, if you are patient, their failure to get your attention will cause the behavior to disappear.

However, be alert that you don't extinguish desirable behavior. When youngsters do something well, they expect to be positively reinforced. Not rewarding them will likely cause them to discontinue the desired behavior.

Discipline

Some educators say we should never discipline young people, but should only reinforce their positive behaviors. They argue that discipline does not work, that it creates hostility and sometimes develops avoidance behaviors that may be more unwholesome than the original problem behavior. It is true that discipline does not always work and that it can create problems when used ineffectively, but when used appropriately, discipline is effective in eliminating undesirable behaviors without creating other undesirable consequences. You must use discipline effectively, because it is impossible to guide athletes through positive reinforcement and extinction alone. Discipline is part of the positive approach when these guidelines are followed:

- Discipline in a corrective way to help athletes improve now and in the future. Don't discipline to retaliate and make yourself feel better.

- Impose discipline in an impersonal way when athletes break team rules or otherwise misbehave. Shouting at or scolding athletes indicates that your attitude is one of revenge.

- Once a good rule has been agreed upon, ensure that athletes who violate it experience the unpleasant consequences of their misbehavior. Don't wave discipline threateningly over their heads. Just do it, but warn an athlete once before disciplining.

- Be consistent in administering discipline.

- Don't discipline using consequences that may cause you guilt. If you can't think of an appropriate consequence right away, tell the player you will talk with him or her after you think about it. You might consider involving the player in designing a consequence.

- Once the discipline is completed, don't make athletes feel they are "in the doghouse." Make them feel that they're valued members of the team again.

- Make sure that what you think is discipline isn't perceived by the athlete as a positive reinforcement—for instance, keeping a player out of doing a certain drill or portion of the practice may be just what the athlete desired.

- Never discipline athletes for making errors when they are playing.

- Never use physical activity—running laps or doing push-ups—as discipline. To do so only causes athletes to resent physical activity, something we want them to learn to enjoy throughout their lives.

- Discipline sparingly. Constant discipline and criticism cause athletes to turn their interests elsewhere and to resent you as well.

Game-Day Coaching

Contests provide the opportunity for your players to show what they've learned in practice. Just as your players' focus shifts on contest days from learning and practicing to *competing*, so your focus shifts from teaching skills to coaching players as they perform those skills in contests. Of course, the contest is a teaching opportunity as well, but the focus is on performing what has been previously learned.

In the last chapter you learned how to teach your players basketball tactics and skills; in this chapter we'll help you coach your players as they execute those tactics and skills in contests. We'll provide important coaching principles that will guide you throughout the game day—before, during, and after the contest.

Before the Contest

Just as you need a practice plan for what you're going to do each practice, you need a game plan for what to do on the day of a game. Many inexperienced coaches focus only on how they will coach during the contest itself, but your preparations to coach should include details that begin well before the first play of the game. In fact, your preparations should begin during the practice before the contest.

Preparations at Practice

During the practice a day or two before the next contest, you should do two things (besides practicing tactics and skills) to prepare your players: Decide on any specific team tactics that you want to employ, and discuss pregame particulars such as what to eat before the game, what to wear, and when to be at the gym.

Deciding Team Tactics

Some coaches see themselves as great military strategists guiding their young warriors to victory on the battlefield. These coaches burn the midnight oil as they devise a complex plan of attack. There are several things wrong with this approach, but we'll point out two errors in terms of deciding team tactics:

1. The decision on team tactics should be made with input from players.

2. Team tactics at this level don't need to be complex.

Perhaps you guessed right on the second point but were surprised by the first. Why should you include your players in deciding tactics? Isn't that the coach's role?

It's the coach's role to help youngsters grow through the sport experience. Giving your athletes a chance to offer input here helps them to learn the game. It gets them involved at a planning level that often is reserved solely for the coach. It gives them a feeling of ownership; they're not just "carrying out orders" of the coach. They're executing the plan of attack that was jointly decided. Youngsters who have a say in how they approach a task often respond with more enthusiasm and motivation.

Don't dampen that enthusiasm and motivation by concocting tactics that are too complex. Keep tactics simple, especially at the younger levels. Focus on maintaining good court balance, penetrating the defense, setting screens to get players open, taking good shots on offense, and cutting off passing lanes on defense.

As you become more familiar with your team's tendencies and abilities, help them focus on specific tactics that will help them play better. For example, if your team has a tendency to stand around and watch the action, emphasize moving more and spreading out the attack. If they are active and moving throughout the game, but not in any cohesive fashion, focus them on setting screens, penetrating the defense, and looking to open up passing lanes.

If you're coaching 12- to 14-year-olds, you might institute certain plays that your team has practiced. These plays should take advantage of your players' strengths. Again, give the players some input into what plays might be employed in a game.

Discussing Precontest Particulars

Players need to know what to do before a contest: what they should eat on game day and when, what clothing they should wear to the game, what equipment they should bring, and what time they should arrive at the gym. Discuss these particulars with them at the practice before a contest. Here are guidelines for discussing these issues.

Pregame Meal. Carbohydrates are easily digested and absorbed and are a ready source of fuel. Players should eat a high-carbohydrate meal ideally about three to four hours before a game to allow the stomach to empty completely. This won't be possible for games held in early morning; in this case, athletes should still eat food high in carbohydrates, such as an English muffin, toast, or cereal, but not so much that their stomachs are full. In addition, athletes' pregame meals shouldn't include foods that are spicy or high in fat content.

Clothing and Equipment. Instruct players to wear their team shirts or uniforms and suitable shoes.

Time to Arrive. Your players will need to adequately warm up before a game, so instruct them to arrive 20 minutes before a game to go through a team warm-up (see "The Warm-Up" on page 56).

Facilities, Equipment, and Support Personnel

Although the site coordinator and referees have responsibilities regarding facilities and equipment, it's wise for you to know what to look for to make sure the contest is safe for the athletes. You should arrive at the court 25 to 30 minutes before game time so you can check the court, check in with the site coordinator and referees, and greet your players as they arrive to warm up. The site coordinator and referees should be checking the facilities and preparing for the contest. If referees aren't arriving before the game when they're supposed to, inform the site coordinator. A facilities checklist includes the following:

Gymnasium Facilities

✔ The stairs and corridors leading to the gym are well lit.

✔ The stairs and corridors are free of obstruction.

✔ The stairs and corridors are in good repair.

✔ Exits are well marked and illuminated.

✔ Exits are free of obstruction.

✔ Uprights and other projections are padded, including the basket standards or poles.

✔ Walls are free of projections.

✔ Windows are located high on the walls.

✔ Wall plugs and light switches are insulated and protected.

✔ Lights are shielded.

✔ Lighting is sufficient to illuminate the playing area well.

✔ The heating/cooling system for the gym is working properly and is monitored regularly.

✔ Ducts, radiators, pipes, and so on are shielded or designed to withstand high impact.

✔ Tamper-free thermostats are housed in impact-resistant covers.

✔ If there is an overhanging track be sure it has secure railings with a minimum height of three feet, six inches.

✔ The track has direction signs posted.

✔ The track is free of obstructions.

✔ Rules for the track are posted.

✔ Projections on the track are padded or illuminated.

✔ Gym equipment is inspected prior to and during each use.

✔ The gym is adequately supervised.

✔ Galleries and viewing areas have been designed to protect small children by blocking their access to the playing area.

✔ The gym (floor, roof, walls, light fixtures, etc.) is inspected on an annual basis for safety and structural deficiencies.

✔ Fire alarms are in good working order.

✔ Fire extinguishers are up to date, with note of last inspection.

✔ Directions are posted for evacuating the gym in case of fire.

Communicating With Parents

The groundwork for your communication with parents will have been laid in the parent orientation program, through which parents learn the best ways to support their kids'—and the whole team's—efforts on the court. As parents gather in the gym before a contest, let them know what the team has been focusing on during the past week and what your goals are for the game. For instance, perhaps you've worked on the "give-and-go" play in practice this week; encourage parents to watch for improvement and success in executing this play and to support the team members as they attempt all tactics and skills. Help parents to judge success not just based on the contest outcome, but on how the kids are improving their performances.

If parents yell at the kids for mistakes made during the game, make disparaging remarks about the officials or opponents, or shout instructions on what tactics to employ, ask them to refrain from making such remarks and to instead be supportive of the team in their comments and actions.

After a contest, briefly and informally assess with parents, as the opportunity arises, how the team did based not on the outcome, but on meeting performance goals and playing to the best of their abilities. Help parents see the contest as a process, not solely as a test that's pass/fail or win/lose. Encourage parents to reinforce that concept at home.

Unplanned Events

Part of being prepared to coach is to expect the unexpected. What do you do if players are late? What if *you* have an emergency and can't make the game or will be late? What if the contest is postponed? Being prepared to handle out-of-the-ordinary circumstances will help you when such unplanned events happen.

If players are late, you may have to adjust your starting lineup. While this may not be a major inconvenience, do stress to your players the importance of being on time for two reasons:

Part of being a member of a team means being committed and responsible to the other members. When players don't show up, or show up late, they break that commitment.

Players need to go through a warm-up to physically prepare for the contest. Skipping the warm-up risks injury. Consider making a team rule stating that players need to show up 20 minutes before a game and go through the complete team warm-up, or they won't start. An emergency might cause *you* to be late or miss a game. In such cases, notify your assistant coach, if you have one, or the league coordinator. If notified in advance, a parent of a player or another volunteer might be able to step in for the contest.

Sometimes a game will be postponed because of inclement weather or for other reasons (such as unsafe court conditions). If the postponement takes place before game day, you'll need to call each member of your team to let him or her know. If it happens while the teams are on the court preparing for the game, gather your team members and tell them the news and why the game is being postponed. Make sure all your players have rides home before you leave—be the last to leave to be sure.

The Warm-Up

Players need to both physically and mentally prepare for a game once they arrive at the court. Physical preparation involves warming up. We've suggested that players arrive 20 minutes before the game to warm up. Conduct the warm-up similar to practice warm-ups, with some brief games that focus on skill practice and stretching.

Players should prepare to do what they will do in the game: dribble, pass, catch, shoot, defend, and rebound. This doesn't mean they spend extensive time on each skill; you can plan two or three brief practice games that encompass all these skills.

After playing a few brief games, your players should stretch. You don't need to deliver any big pep talk, but you can help your players mentally prepare as they stretch by reminding them of the following:

⊙ The tactics and skills they've been working on in recent practices, especially focusing their attention on what they've been doing well.

⊙ Focusing on their strengths.

⊙ The team tactics you decided on in your previous practice.

⊙ Performing the tactics and skills to the best of their individual abilities and playing together as a team.

⊙ Playing hard and smart and having fun!

During the Contest

The list you just read goes a long way toward defining your focus for coaching during the contest. Throughout the game, you'll keep the game in proper perspective and help your players do the same. You'll observe how your players execute tactics and skills and how well they play together. You'll make tactical decisions in a number of areas. You'll model appropriate behavior on the bench, showing respect for opponents and officials, and demand the same of your athletes. You'll watch out for your athletes' physical safety and psychological welfare, in terms of building their self-esteem and helping them manage stress and anxiety.

Proper Perspective

Winning games is the short-term goal of your basketball program; helping your players learn the tactics, skills, and rules of basketball, how to become fit, and how to be good sports in basketball and in life is the long-term goal. Your young athletes are "winning" when they are becoming better human beings through their participation in basketball. Keep that perspective in mind when you coach. *You* have the privilege of setting the tone for how your team approaches the game. Keep winning and all aspects of the competition in proper perspective, and your young charges will likely follow suit.

Tactical Decisions

While you aren't called upon to be a great military strategist, you are called upon to make tactical decisions in several areas throughout a contest. You'll make decisions about who starts the game and when to enter substitutes, about making slight adjustments to your team's tactics, and about correcting players' performance errors or leaving the correction for the next practice.

Starting and Substituting Players

In considering playing time at the younger levels, make sure that everyone on the team gets to play at least half of each game. This should be your guiding principle as you consider starting and substitution patterns. We suggest you consider two options in substituting players:

Substituting Individually. Replace one player with another. This offers you a lot of latitude in deciding who goes in when, and it gives you the greatest mix of players throughout the game, but it can be hard to keep track of playing time (this could be made easier by assigning an assistant or a parent to this task).

Substituting by Quarters. The advantage here is that you can easily track playing time, and players know how long they will be in before they might be replaced.

Adjusting Team Tactics

At the 8 to 9 and 10 to 11 age levels, you probably won't adjust your team tactics too significantly during a game; rather, you'll focus on the basic tactics in general and emphasize during breaks which tactics your team needs to work on in particular.

However, coaches of 12- to 14-year-olds might have cause to make tactical adjustments to improve their team's chances of performing well and winning. As games progress, assess your opponents' style of play and tactics, and make adjustments that are appropriate—that is, that your players are prepared for. For example, if your opponent likes to run a lot and is beating your team on fast breaks, you might make sure you have at least a few quick players who can get back on defense.

However, don't stress tactics too much during a game. Doing so can take the fun out of the game for the players. If you don't trust your memory, carry a pen and notepad to note which team tactics and individual skills need attention in the next practice.

Correcting Players' Errors

In chapter 5 you learned about two types of errors: learning errors and performance errors. Learning errors are ones that occur because athletes don't know how to perform a skill. Athletes make performance errors not because they don't know how to do the skill, but because they make a mistake in executing what they do know.

Sometimes it's not easy to tell which type of error athletes are making. Knowing your athletes' capabilities helps you to know whether they know the skill and are simply making mistakes in executing it or whether they don't really know how to perform the skill. If they are making learning errors—that is, they don't know how to perform the skills—you'll need to make note of this and teach them at the next practice. Game time is not the time to teach skills.

If they are making performance errors, however, you can help players correct those errors during a game. Players who make performance errors often do so because they have a lapse in concentration or motivation—or they are simply demonstrating the human quality of sometimes doing things incorrectly. A word of encouragement to concentrate more may help. If you do correct a performance error during a contest, do so in a quiet, controlled, and positive tone of voice during a break or when the player is on the bench with you.

For those making performance errors, you have to decide if it is just the occasional error anyone makes or an expected error for a youngster at that stage of development. If that is the case, then the player may appreciate your not commenting on the mistake. The player knows it was a mistake and knows how to correct it. On the other hand, perhaps an encouraging word and a "coaching cue" (such as "Remember to follow through on your shots") may be just what the athlete needs. Knowing the players and what to say is very much a part of the "art" of coaching.

Coach's and Players' Behavior

Another aspect of coaching on game day is managing behavior—both yours and your athletes'. The two are closely connected.

Your Conduct

You very much influence your players' behavior before, during, and after a contest. If you're up, your players are more likely to be up. If you're anxious, they'll notice and the anxiety can be contagious. If you're negative, they'll respond with worry. If you're positive, they'll play with more enjoyment. If you're constantly yelling instructions or commenting on mistakes and errors, it will be difficult for players to concentrate. Instead, let players get into the flow of the game.

The focus should be on positive competition and on having fun. A coach who overorganizes everything and dominates a game from the sideline is definitely *not* making the contest fun.

So how should you conduct yourself on the bench? Here are a few pointers:

- Be calm, in control, and supportive of your players.
- Encourage players often, but instruct during play sparingly. Players should be focusing on their performance during a game, not on instructions shouted from the bench.
- If you need to instruct a player, do so when you're both on the bench, in an unobtrusive manner. Never yell at players for making a mistake. Instead, briefly demonstrate or remind them of the correct technique and encourage them.

Remember, you're not playing for an Olympic gold medal! In this program, basketball competitions are designed to help players develop their skills and themselves—and to have fun. So coach in a manner at games that helps your players do those things.

Players' Conduct

You're responsible for keeping your players under control. Do so by setting a good example and by disciplining when necessary. Set team rules of good behavior. If players attempt to cheat, fight, argue, badger, yell disparaging remarks, and the like, it is your responsibility to correct the misbehavior. Consider team rules in these areas of game conduct:

- Players' language
- Players' behavior
- Interactions with referees
- Discipline for misbehavior
- Dress code for competitions

Players' Physical Safety

We devoted all of chapter 3 to discussing how to provide for players' safety, but it's worth noting here that safety during contests can be affected by how referees are calling the rules. If they aren't calling rules correctly, and this risks injury to your players, you must intervene. Voice your concern in a respectful manner and in a way that places the emphasis where it should be: on the athletes' safety. One of the referees' main responsibilities is to provide for athletes' safety; you are not adversaries here. Don't hesitate to address an issue of safety with a referee when the need arises.

Players' Psychological Welfare

Athletes often attach their self-worth to winning and losing. This idea is fueled by coaches, parents, peers, and society, who place great emphasis on winning. Players become anxious when they're uncertain if they can meet the expectations of others or of themselves when meeting these expectations is important to them.

If you place too much importance on the game or cause your athletes to doubt their abilities, they will become anxious about the outcome and their performance. If your players look uptight and anxious during a contest, find ways to reduce both the uncertainties about how their performance will be evaluated and the importance they are attaching to the game. Help athletes focus on realistic personal goals—

goals that are reachable and measurable and that will help them improve their performance. Another way to reduce anxiety on game day is to stay away from emotional pregame pep talks. We provided guidance earlier in what to address before the game.

When coaching during contests, remember that the most important outcome from playing basketball is to build or enhance players' self-worth. Keep that firmly in mind, and strive to make every coaching decision promote your athletes' self-worth.

Opponents and Referees

Respect opponents and referees. Without them, you wouldn't have a competition. Referees help provide a fair and safe experience for athletes and, as appropriate, help them learn the game. Opponents provide opportunities for your team to test itself, improve, and excel.

You and your team should show respect for opponents by giving your best efforts. You owe them this. Showing respect doesn't necessarily mean being "nice" to your opponents, though it does mean being civil.

Don't allow your players to "trash talk" or taunt an opponent. Such behavior is disrespectful to the spirit of the competition and to the opponent. Immediately remove a player from a contest if he or she disobeys your orders in this area.

Remember that referees are quite often teenagers—in many cases not much older than the players themselves. The level of officiating should be commensurate to the level of play. In other words, don't expect perfection from referees any more than you do from your own players. Especially at the younger levels, they *won't* make every call, because to do so would stop the contest every 10 seconds.

After the Contest

When the game is over, join your team in congratulating the coaches and players of the opposing team, then be sure to thank the referees. Check on any injuries players sustained and let players know how to care for them. Be prepared to speak with the referees about any problems that occurred during the game. Then hold a brief Team Circle, as explained in a moment, to ensure your players are on an even keel, whether they won or lost.

Winning With Class, Losing With Dignity

When celebrating a victory, make sure your team does so in a way that doesn't show disrespect for the opponents. It's fine and appropriate to be happy and celebrate a win, but don't allow your players to taunt the opponents or boast about their victory. Keep winning in perspective. Winning and losing are a part of life, not just a part of sport. If players can handle both equally well, they'll be successful in whatever they do.

Athletes are competitors, and competitors will be disappointed in defeat. If your team has made a winning effort, let them know that. After a loss, help them keep their chins up and maintain a positive attitude that will carry over into the next practice and contest.

Team Circle

If your players have performed well in a game, compliment them and congratulate them immediately afterward. Tell them specifically what they did well, whether they won or lost. This will reinforce their desire to repeat their good performances.

Don't criticize individual players for poor performances in front of teammates. Help players improve their skills, but do so in the next practice, not immediately after a game.

The postgame Team Circle isn't the time to go over tactical problems and adjustments. The players are either so happy after a win or so dejected after a loss that they won't absorb much tactical information immediately following a game. Your first concern should be your players' attitudes and mental well-being. You don't want them to be too high after a win or too low after a loss. This is the time you can be most influential in keeping the outcome in perspective and keeping them on an even keel.

Finally, make sure your players have transportation home. Be the last one to leave in order to help if transportation falls through and to ensure full supervision of players before they leave.

Rules and Equipment

This is where we'll introduce you to some of the basic rules of basketball. We won't try to cover all the rules of the game, but rather we'll give you what you need to work with players who are 8 to 14 years old. We'll give you information on equipment, court size and markings, player positions, actions to start and restart the game, fouls, violations, and scoring. We'll recommend rules modifications to make the sport more appropriate for youngsters. In a short section at the end of the chapter we'll show you the officiating signals for basketball.

Equipment, Court, and Game Length

Basketball requires very little player equipment. Players should wear basketball shoes so they have proper traction on the court. They should wear clothing such as athletic shorts and tank tops or loose-fitting shirts so they have the freedom of movement needed to run, jump, and shoot. Players may choose to wear safety glasses or goggles to protect their eyes from injury. Also, if desired, players who have conditions affecting the knees or elbows may want to wear soft pads to protect them.

Players may *not* wear jewelry during games. In table 7.1 we present rules that cover many of the basics of the game. Figure 7.1 shows standard basketball court markings.

Several areas of the court are referred to with special basketball terminology:

Frontcourt—refers to the half of the court where your team's offensive basket is located.

Backcourt—includes the midcourt line and the half of the court where your opponent's basket is located.

Table 7.1 Rule Modifications for Basketball

	8- to 9-year-olds	10- to 11-year-olds	12- to 14-year-olds
Players on team	9	9	9
Ball size	Junior (#5)	Women's (#6)	Regulation (#7)
Court size	Short court	Short court	Full court
Free-throw distance	9 ft	9 ft	12-15 ft
Game length	24 min	24 min	32 min
Time-outs	4	4	4
Players on court	5 v 5	5 v 5	5 v 5
Basket height	7 ft	8 ft	9-10 ft

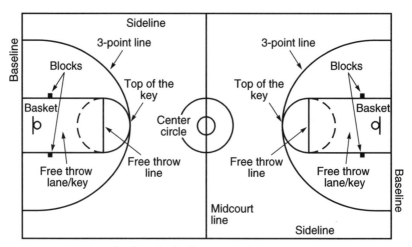

Figure 7.1 Standard basketball court markings.

Blocks—square markings six feet from the baseline on each side of the lane.

Perimeter—the area outside the three-second lane area.

Three-point line—a semicircle that is 19 feet, 9 inches from the basket at all points. Shots that are made from behind this line count for three points instead of two.

Three-second lane—an area that extends from the baseline under the basket to the free-throw line; it's also called the *key*.

Top of the key—the semicircle that extends beyond the free-throw line.

Player Positions

Basketball is usually played with five players on a team. Some leagues for 8- and 9-year-olds might consider playing 3 v 3 or 4 v 4, and some leagues for 10- and 11-year-olds might consider playing 4 v 4. We do recommend that 12- and 14-year-olds play 5 v 5 in competitions. Each player is assigned a position, which is often referred to by number (1 through 5). The types of positions are guard, forward, and center.

Guards

Guards usually are the best ball handlers and outside shooters on the team. They tend to be shorter and quicker than the other players and have good dribbling and passing skills. Guards play farthest from the basket, on the perimeter.

A basketball team usually has two guards in the game at all times. The point guard, who is in the #1 position, is played by the team's best dribbler and passer. The second guard is the off-guard, who is in the #2 position. He or she is often the team's best long-range shooter and second-best dribbler.

Forwards

Forwards typically are taller than guards and play closer to the basket. They should be able to shoot the ball accurately from within 12 feet of the basket and rebound the ball when shots are missed.

A team usually plays with two forwards in its lineup. The small forward (also referred to as the wing) is in the #3 position. This position often is filled by the most versatile and athletic member of the team. The small forward must be able to play in the lane and on the perimeter on offense, and to guard small and quick or big and strong opponents on defense. The other forward position is the big forward, or the #4 position. This is a good spot to assign to one of your bigger players and better rebounders—who can also shoot the ball from anywhere in the lane area.

Center

The center, or #5 position (also called the *post position*), is frequently the tallest or biggest player on the team. That extra size is helpful in maneuvering for shots or rebounds around the basket. A tall center can also make it difficult for opposing teams to shoot near the basket. A center should have "soft" hands to catch the passes thrown into the lane area by guards and forwards. Most basketball teams designate one player on the court as their center.

Starting and Restarting the Game

In regulation play, a jump ball at center court is used to start games and overtime periods, which are played when teams are tied at the end of regulation time. During jump balls, the official tosses up the ball between two players, usually each team's center or best leaper. Each player attempts to tip the ball to a teammate (who must be outside of the center circle) to gain possession of the ball. Another jump ball situation is simultaneous possession of the ball by players from opposing teams. In this case, teams alternate possession; the team that did not win the first jump ball takes the ball out of bounds in the next jump ball situation.

Play stops during intermissions and time-outs, but also when the ball goes out of bounds and when an official calls a violation or a foul. The clock restarts when the ball is touched following an inbounds pass or a missed free throw.

Fouls

Basketball is a contact sport, with players in close proximity and in constant motion. The rules of the game discourage rough play or tactics that allow a team to gain an advantage through brute force. Therefore, fouls are called when officials see illegal physical contact between two or more players based on these general principles:

- The first player to establish position (to become stationary or set) on the court has priority rights to that position.
- A body part cannot be extended into the path of an opponent.
- The player who moves into the path of an opponent—especially an airborne opponent—when contact occurs is responsible for the contact.
- All players have the right to the space extending straight up from their feet on the floor. This is called the *principle of verticality*.

Types of Fouls

Based on the general principles concerning player contact, these specific fouls are called in a regulation game:

Blocking—physically impeding the progress of another player who is still moving.

Charging—running into or pushing a defender who is stationary.

Hand-checking—using the hands to check the progress of an offensive player when that player is in front of the defender who is using the hands.

Holding—restricting the movement of an opponent.

Illegal screen—a form of blocking in which the player setting the screen is still moving when the defender makes contact.

Over-the-back—infringing on the vertical plane of, and making contact with, a player who is in position and attempting to rebound.

Pushing—impeding the progress or otherwise moving a player by pushing or shoving.

Reaching in—extending an arm and making contact with a ball handler in an attempt to steal the ball.

Tripping—extending a leg or foot and causing an opponent to lose balance or fall.

The fouls just described are called *personal fouls*. This list covers most common ones, although there are others. Another type of foul is a *shooting foul*, in which a defender makes contact with a player who is shooting the basketball. Emphasize to your players the importance of keeping hands off the shooter, establishing position, using the feet to maintain position rather than reaching in with the hands, and not attempting to rebound over an opponent who has established position.

Other types of fouls exist, such as a *technical foul;* this is a foul that does not involve contact with the opponent while the ball is alive (use of profanity, delay of game, unsporting conduct). *Intentional* and *flagrant fouls* relate to extreme behaviors and should hopefully not come up with your players. If they do, players who are guilty of unsporting conduct during a game are usually ejected, assessed a technical foul, and should be counseled by the coach. In such a case the opposing team is awarded two free throws and possession of the ball.

Consequences of Fouls

A team that fouls too much pays for it. Fouls carry with them increasingly severe penalties. A player who has five fouls must sit for the remainder of the game. In regulation play, a team that has more than a specified number of fouls in a quarter or half gives the opposing team a bonus situation: The member of the team who was fouled is allowed to shoot free throws. If the foul is a nonshooting foul, the player shoots one free throw and, if he or she makes it, shoots a second one (this is called *one-and-one*). If the foul is made during shooting, then the player shoots two free throws. Table 7.2 lists the types of fouls and their consequences.

Violations

Turnovers—the loss of the ball to the defense—caused by violations will be one of your continuing frustrations as a basketball coach. Violations can be categorized as ballhandling violations and clock violations.

Here are common violations committed by ball handlers:

Double dribble—resuming dribbling after having stopped (when no defender interrupts the player's possession of the ball) or dribbling with both hands at the same time.

Over-and-back—the return of the ball to the backcourt when last touched by an offensive player in the frontcourt.

Table 7.2   **Fouls and Consequences**

Type of foul	Team fouled in bonus	Penalty
Personal	No	Ball out-of-bounds
Personal	Yes	One-on-one free throws
Shooting	Yes/No	Two free throws
Technical	Yes/No	Two free throws and ball out-of-bounds
Intentional	Yes/No	Two free throws and ball out-of-bounds
Flagrant	Yes/No	Two free throws, fouler is disqualified, ball out-of-bounds

Traveling—taking more than one step without dribbling; also called *carrying the ball* or *palming the ball,* as a player turns the ball a complete rotation in the hand between dribbles.

Here are common clock violations:

Inbounds—on any inbounds play the thrower-in has 5 seconds to release the ball.

Lane—an offensive player cannot be in the lane (in the key) for more than 3 seconds at a time.

Backcourt—a team must advance the ball into its frontcourt within 10 seconds after gaining possession in the backcourt.

Shot clock—the ball must leave an offensive player's hands before the shot clock expires. The ball must subsequently hit the rim on that shot or it will be a violation.

Table 7.3 shows our recommendations for modifying the rules for these violations. Table 7.4 shows modified rules for defensive play.

Table 7.3 Modified Rules for Violations

Violation	8- to 9-year-olds	10- to 11-year-olds	12- to 14-year-olds
Double dribble	Allow one violation per player possession; gradually tighten up this allowance.	Allow one violation per player possession; gradually tighten up this allowance.	Call.
Over-and-back	Don't call.	Don't call.	Call.
Traveling	Give an extra step for starting and stopping; gradually tighten up this allowance.	Give an extra step for starting and stopping; gradually tighten up this allowance.	Call.
Inbounds (5-sec)	Don't call.	Give warnings early in season; call after mid-season.	Call.

(continued)

Table 7.3   (continued)

Violation	8- to 9-year-olds	10- to 11-year-olds	12- to 14-year-olds
Lane (3-sec)	Don't call.	Give warnings early in season; call after mid-season.	Call.
Backcourt (10-sec)	Don't call.	Give warnings early in season; call after mid-season.	Call.
Shot clock	Don't use.	Don't use.	Don't use.

Table 7.4   Modified Rules for Defensive Play

Defense may...	8- to 9-year-olds	10- to 11-year-olds	12- to 14-year-olds
Use player-to-player defense	Yes	Yes	Yes
Use zone defense	No	No	No
Use full-court press	No	No	No
Strip ball-handler of ball	No	Yes	Yes
Draw charges	No	No	Yes

Scoring

In regulation play, teams are awarded 2 points for every field goal inside the three-point line, and 3 points for shots made beyond the three-point stripe. A successful free throw is worth 1 point. (Players may not enter the lane until the free throw has hit the rim. If the free throw doesn't hit the rim, the ball is awarded to the opposing team out of bounds.) The team that scores the most points over the course of the game is the winner.

Officiating

Games are officiated by one or two officials who should know the rules and enforce them to ensure a safe, fair, and fun contest. Officials should also require good sporting behavior from all players and coaches. You can be a big help to officials by respecting their efforts and emphasizing to your players the need to play with respect for the rules. Figure 7.2a-t shows some common officiating signals. Familiarize yourself with these signals and explain them to your players.

(continued)

Figure 7.2   Some signals commonly used by umpires are *(a)* starting clock, *(b)* stopping clock for jump ball, *(c)* beckoning a sub in on a dead ball, *(d)* stopping clock for foul, *(e)* scoring one point, and *(f)* scoring two points,

Figure 7.2 *(continued)* *(g)* scoring three points, *(h)* blocking, *(i)* bonus situation, *(j)* over-and-back or carrying the ball, *(k)* pushing, *(l)* illegal use of hands,

Figure 7.2 *(continued)* *(m)* technical foul, *(n)* three-second violation, *(o)* designating out-of-bounds spot, *(p)* traveling, *(q)* holding, *(r)* no score, *(s)* illegal dribble, and *(t)* hand check.

Tactics and Skills

As your athletes play games in practice, their experiences in these games—and your subsequent discussions with them about their experiences—will lead them to the tactics and skills that they need to develop to succeed. In the games approach to teaching basketball, tactics and skills go hand in hand.

In this chapter, we'll provide information for you to teach your players team tactics and individual offensive and defensive skills. We'll also include suggestions for identifying and correcting common errors. Remember to use the IDEA approach to teaching skills—Introduce, Demonstrate, Explain the skill, and Attend to players as they practice the skill. For a refresher on IDEA, see chapter 5. If you aren't familiar with basketball skills, rent or purchase a video to see the skills performed. You may also find advanced books on skills helpful.

We've only provided information about the basics of basketball in this book. As your players advance in their basketball skills, you'll need to advance in your knowledge as a coach. You can do so by learning from your experiences, by watching and talking with more experienced coaches, and by studying advanced resources.

Offensive Tactics

In basketball, the offensive team's primary objective is to move the ball effectively so that they can score. A secondary goal is to maintain ball possession so that the opposing team cannot score. The following tactics will help your team accomplish these goals.

Creating Passing Lanes

To move the ball effectively, your team needs to move well without the ball and create passing lanes, which are spaces between offensive players where a pass can be made. Players create passing lanes by using cuts and screens, by maintaining space and court balance, by keeping the middle open, and by quickly moving to a vacated spot. We'll address cuts and screens later in this chapter. Here we'll take a closer look at maintaining court balance, keeping the middle open, and moving to a vacated spot.

⊙ **Maintaining court balance.** Players should start in an open formation about 12 to 15 feet apart. They should be spaced high at the top, wide on the wing, and at the midpoint between the basket and corner on the baseline.

⊙ **Keeping the middle open.** When a player cuts to the basket and doesn't receive a pass, he should continue through and fill an open spot on the side of the court with fewer players. This will keep the middle open and the floor balanced. Players shouldn't stay in the post area for more than one count.

⊙ **Moving to a vacated spot.** The person who is the next player away from a cutting player should move quickly to the vacated spot (see figure 8.1). This is especially important when the player has cut from the point or top position. When replacing the player at the point, the new player should swing wide above the three-point line, creating a better passing angle from the wing.

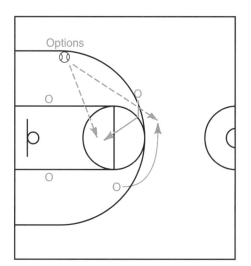

Figure 8.1   The player who is the next player away from a cutting player should quickly move to the vacated spot.

Passing Lane Game

ROOM TO MOVE

Goal

To create passing lanes and move to open space.

Description

Play 3 v 2. The offensive players move to open space. Players pass and then move to a place on the court—point, wing, baseline, low post—that is adjacent to the ball (see figure 8.2). The focus is on constant ball movement and moving to open space. Players can dribble, too, but the emphasis is on little dribbling and crisp passing. Players must make 10 passes; after the 10th pass, they can shoot and continue to shoot until they score or the defense rebounds.

Give one point for each pass successfully received and one point for a basket. Once a basket is made or the defense rebounds, begin again, this time with the two defenders moving to offense.

To make the game easier:

⊙ Play 3 v 1.

To make the game more challenging:

⊙ Play 3 v 3.

⊙ Allow no dribbling.

(continued)

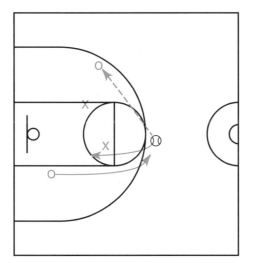

Figure 8.2 Creating passing lanes.

Setting Screens

Screens may be set for a player with or without the ball; they help players get open for passes and shots. An offensive player who sets a screen, or pick, positions herself as a stationary barrier on one side of a teammate's defender, blocking the defender's path as the teammate cuts around the screen to get open (see figure 8.3). The screening player stands erect with feet planted shoulder-width apart and arms down to the sides or crossed at the chest. The screen should be set perpendicular to the path of the defender. Against good defensive teams the cutter may often be covered, but the screener will often be open to receive a pass after setting the screen.

Direct players to "screen away" from the ball, meaning that they should set screens for teammates who are on the opposite (weak) side of the court from the ball. That way the player for whom the screen is set will be moving toward the passer after coming off the screen. Players should cut right by (actually brushing by) the screeners.

Error Detection and Correction for Screening

ERROR The player sets moving screens, which are illegal.

CORRECTION The player should use a wide, two-footed jump stop (see page 105) to avoid an illegal moving screen before his or her teammate cuts. The screener should keep his or her arms and knees in as the defender fights through.

Figure 8.3   Proper technique for setting a screen.

Setting Screens Game

SCREEN DOOR

Goal

To set effective screens to free up teammates.

Description

Play 3 v 2. The offense must complete three passes before attempting a screen. With the ballhandler out on top with the ball, one teammate sets a screen for the other teammate, who cuts around the screen and looks for a pass from the ballhandler (see figure 8.4). The ballhandler can call out, "PR" (which signals to set a pick on the right side) or "PL" (which signals to set a pick on the left side), or the teammates can move on their own without the call.

Give the offense five possessions, and give them two points for each successful screen and one point for each basket scored directly off the screen. (A screen is successful if it frees the teammate from her defender.) Reset the play after a shot is taken, whether the ball goes in or not.

(continued)

Screen Door *(continued)*

To make the game easier:

◎ Play 3 v 1.

◎ Play a "cold" defense—one in which defenders are passive and moving at about half speed.

To make the game more challenging:

◎ Play 3 v 3.

◎ Play a "hot" defense—the defenders play all out.

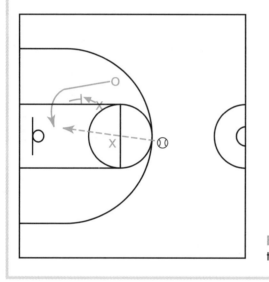

Figure 8.4 Setting a screen to free a teammate.

Transition Game

The fast break usually develops after a rebound, steal, or possibly after a made basket, and is the fastest way to make the transition from defense to offense. As soon as the defense gains control of the ball, they use the outlet pass or dribble to start the break—passing being the first option, because it moves the ball faster. On a rebound, the rebounder should pivot toward the wing area on that side of the court and hit the outlet (#1, #2, or #3 player). The player receiving the pass gets the ball to the middle of the court by either passing or dribbling; teammates should fill the lanes on either side as they proceed down the court. The player with the ball in the middle wants to get to the free-throw line under control before passing to either lane for a shot or short drive.

It's important to stay spread out and run at top speed under control during the fast break. The last two players down the floor are called trailers (usually #4 and #5). They cut directly to the blocks on either side, looking for a pass from one of the outside lanes. Trailers often get passes on the blocks from the right or left lane cutters when the defense moves out to cover them on the wings. An example of the fast break is shown in figure 8.5.

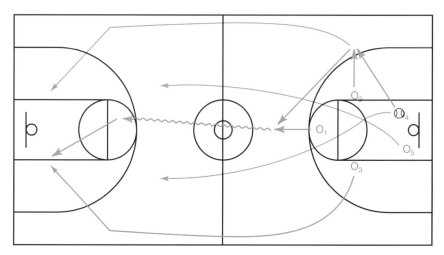

Figure 8.5 Fast break.

Error Detection and Correction for the Fast Break

ERROR   Players anticipate that a teammate will gain possession, and they run away from the ball to start the fast break before obtaining possession.

CORRECTION   Players must first gain possession of the ball before starting their fast break.

ERROR   After rebounding, a player is trapped or is in a congested area and unable to make the outlet pass.

CORRECTION   The player should use one or two power dribbles up the middle and then look to pass.

A point guard who sees that the rebounder is unable to make the outlet pass should come back to the rebounder to receive a short pass or handoff. The point guard should call out, "Ball!" to demand the ball.

Transition Game

LIFE IN THE FAST LANE

Goal

To convert fast-break opportunities into baskets.

Description

Play 2 v 4. The defense allows one of the two offensive players to take a shot to begin the game. Instruct the offense to purposely miss the shot. (A made shot is given back to the offense to shoot again with no points scored.) The defense rebounds and runs a fast break, making the outlet pass and filling the lanes (see figure 8.6). The defense attempts to stop the fast break. Give two points for a well-executed break and an additional point for finishing it off with a bucket. Then begin the game again at the end just scored on.

To make the game easier:

 ⊙ Play 1 v 4 or 1 v 3.

To make the game more challenging:

 ⊙ Play 3 v 4 or 4 v 4.
 ⊙ Allow no dribbling.

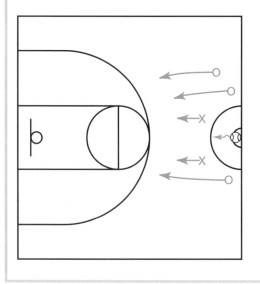

Figure 8.6   Filling the lanes on a fast break.

Give-and-Go

The give-and-go is the most basic play in basketball. The name comes from the action: One player gives (passes) the ball to a teammate and goes (cuts) to the basket, looking to receive a return pass for a layup (see figure 8.7, page 84). The give-and-go exemplifies team play. By passing the ball and then moving without it, the player creates an opportunity to score on a return pass. If the player does not get open on the cut, the movement at least gives the teammate a better opportunity to initiate a one-on-one move, because the cutter's defender will be in a less advantageous position to give defensive help.

After a player initiates the give-and-go with a pass (see figure 8.7a), he or she reads the defender's position before cutting to the basket. If the defender moves with the passer, continuing to guard closely, the passer should simply make a hard cut to the basket. However, if the defender drops off, moving toward the ball on the pass, the passer should set the defender up with a fake before cutting (see figure 8.7b). The passer should fake by taking a step or two away from the ball, and then, as the defender moves with the passer, the passer should make a sharp cut in front of the defender toward the basket (see figure 8.7c). The passer can also fake by taking a step or two toward the ball, then make a sharp cut behind the defender. This is called a backdoor cut. The key is for players to read their defenders to know which type of cut—a front cut or a backdoor cut—will be most effective.

Error Detection and Correction for the Give-and-Go

ERROR   Players do not have enough space to get open.

CORRECTION   At the point, start the give-and-go at least a step above the free-throw circle; on the wing, start the give-and-go a step above the foul line extended.

ERROR   After passing, a player doesn't read defender's position and rushes his cut.

CORRECTION   The player should read the defender's position; if he is closely guarded, he should cut hard. If the defender moves back and toward the ball, the player should fake away or toward the ball before cutting.

a

b

c

Figure 8.7 The give-and-go.

Give-and-Go Game

RETURN TO SENDER

Goal

To score off of the give-and-go play.

Description

Play 3 v 3. The offensive players look to pass and then cut to the basket, holding their hands up and looking for a return pass (see figure 8.8). Shots must be taken within five feet of the basket. Baskets scored directly off the give-and-go count for two points; other baskets count one point. Reset the offense after each play. Give the offense five opportunities to run give-and-gos; then switch offense and defense.

To make the game easier:

⊙ Play 3 v 2.

⊙ Play a "cold" defense (passive, about half speed).

To make the game more challenging:

⊙ Play a "hot" defense (aggressive and full speed).

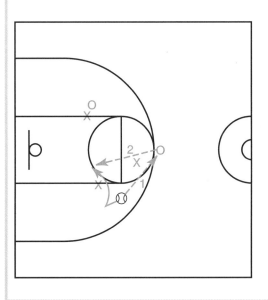

Figure 8.8   Executing the give-and-go.

Pick-and-Roll

The pick-and-roll is another basic play that has always been a part of basketball. Its name, like that of the give-and-go, comes from the action of the play. A player sets a pick (screen) for a teammate (see figure 8.9a) who dribbles by it for an outside shot or a drive. The screener then rolls toward the basket (see figure 8.9b), looking for a pass from the dribbler for a layup. It's important that the dribbler take at least two dribbles beyond the screen to create space for the pass to the screener who rolls to the basket.

a

b

Figure 8.9 The pick-and-roll.

Error Detection and Correction for the Pick-and-Roll

ERROR   A player doesn't wait for the pick to be set. The player dribbles off the pick while her teammate is still moving, causing a foul on the teammate for setting an illegal moving block.

CORRECTION   Before using the pick, the player must wait until a legal pick is set and until she has read the defender's position.

ERROR   As a player rolls or cuts, he does not give a target with his lead hand.

CORRECTION   After making a roll or cut, the player should get his lead hand up for a target (see figure 8.10).

Pick-and-Roll Game

PICKIN' FOR POINTS

Goal

To score off of the pick-and-roll play.

Description

Play 3 v 2. The offense must complete three passes before attempting a pick-and-roll. With the ballhandler out on top with the ball, one teammate sets a screen for the other teammate, then rolls to the basket, hand up, to receive a pass (see figure 8.10). All shots must be shot off of a pick-and-roll.

Give the offense five possessions, and give them two points for each successful pick-and-roll that ends in a basket. Reset the play after a shot is taken, whether the ball goes in or not. Switch teams after five plays.

To make the game easier:

⊙ Play 3 v 1.

⊙ Play a "cold" defense (passive and about half speed).

(continued)

Pickin' for Points *(continued)*

To make the game more challenging:

⊙ Play 3 v 3.

⊙ Play a "hot" defense (all out).

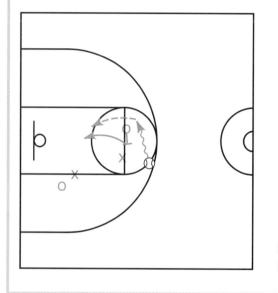

Figure 8.10 Executing the pick-and roll.

Inbounds Plays

Design most of your inbounds plays to create easy scoring opportunities when your team puts the ball in play from underneath your basket. Keep the plays simple and limit them to just a few. Consider aligning in the same manner for each play so that your players aren't confused about where to position themselves and the defense isn't tipped off by a change in formation.

Two options for offensive inbounds plays are shown in figure 8.11a and b. But you can design your own plays or use some from other coaches. The key is to have a good passer inbound the ball and for the rest of the team to cut hard to their designated spots.

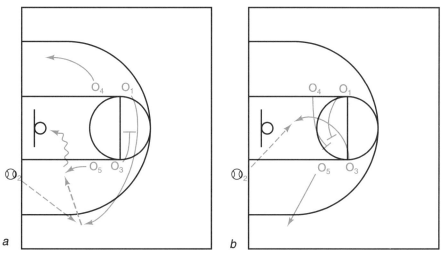

Figure 8.11   Offensive inbounds plays.

Error Detection and Correction for Inbounds Plays

ERROR   Players aren't getting open for passes.

CORRECTION   Players need to know their roles and make quick moves and sharp cuts, presenting targets with their hands to receive the ball.

Inbounds Play Game

5 SECONDS TO GO

Goal

To score off of an inbounds play.

Description

Play 5 v 3. Run one or more of your inbounds plays. Give the offense five attempts to score on inbounds plays, and one point for each basket scored before five seconds elapse. Then switch teams.

(continued)

5 Seconds to Go *(continued)*

To make the game easier:

⊙ Play a "cold" defense (passive and about half speed).

To make the game more challenging:

⊙ Play 5 v 4 or 5 v 5.

⊙ Play a "hot" defense (all out).

Jump Balls

How players are positioned for a jump ball depends on whether your team has the better chance of controlling the tip—that is, winning the jump ball. If the player jumping for you has the advantage, your team should align in an offensive formation and attempt to score off the play (see figure 8.12). If, however, it appears that the opposing team will gain possession, a defensive setup is appropriate (see figure 8.13). The jumper should tip the ball to an open spot where two teammates are next to each other without an opponent in between.

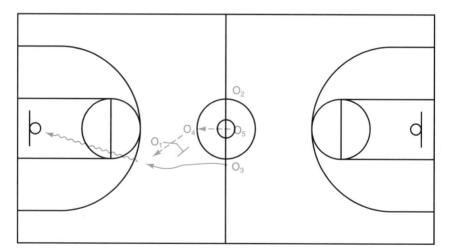

Figures 8.12   Offensive formation for a jump ball.

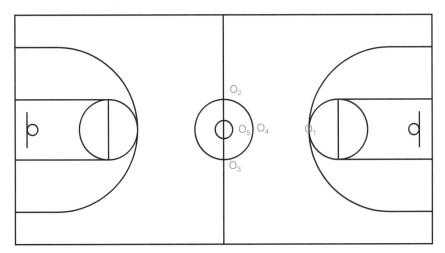

Figures 8.13   Defensive formation for a jump ball.

Defensive Tactics

Playing good defense involves using correct technique and working together with teammates. Good defense inhibits opponents by limiting the number of uncontested shots. Good team defense not only reduces scoring opportunities for the opponents, but it also opens them to your team.

Teams with less-than-average offensive talent can be successful by playing hard, intelligent team defense. Defense is more consistent than offense because it is based mostly on desire and effort. Players might have an off game in shooting, but they should never have an off game on defense, because they control their desire and effort.

In this section we'll focus on three aspects of defensive tactics: defending against screens, cutting off passing lanes, and helping out. Later in the chapter we'll address the individual skills of playing defense on the ball and off the ball.

Defending Against Screens

To defend against screens, players need to communicate and help one another. The defender on the opponent who is setting the screen must alert the defender being screened by calling out the direction of the screen: "Screen right!" or "Screen left!" Three ways to defend against a screen are to fight over the top of the screen, to slide behind it, and to switch.

Fight Over the Top

A player should fight over the top of a screen when there is room for the defender to get between the screener and the screener's teammate. The defender whom the screen was set on should let the teammate know to stay with his opponent by shouting, "Through!" or "Over!" The defender being screened should work to get through the screen by first getting a foot over the screen and then the remainder of the body (see figure 8.14).

Slide Behind

When an opponent sets a screen on a player guarding a quick driver or when the action is outside the opponent's shooting range (see figure 8.15a), the player being screened should slide behind the screen (see

Figure 8.14 Fighting over the top of a screen.

figure 8.15b). In this case the player being screened slides between the screener and the teammate guarding the screener (this teammate should step back to allow the player to slide through).

a

b

Figure 8.15   Sliding behind a screen.

Switch

When teammates are of equal size and defensive ability, they can switch opponents (see figure 8.16a). If size and defensive ability differ, switching should be the last option, as it allows the offense to take advantage of a mismatch. Players who switch should call out the screen by yelling, "Switch!" (see figure 8.16b). As players switch, one player must aggressively get in position to deny a pass to the cutter (the screener who rolls to the basket) while the other player gets in position on the ball side of the screener (see figure 8.16c).

a

b

c

Figure 8.16   Switching on a screen.

Defending Against Screens Game

CUT OFF AT THE PASS

Goal

To defend against screens.

Description

Play 2 v 2, 3 v 3, or 4 v 4. The offense must use screens in setting up plays. If the defense defends well against a screen (that is, no advantage is gained; see figure 8.17), the defense is awarded one point. If the offense gains an advantage on the screen, the defense loses one point. If the offense scores directly off of the screen, the defense loses two points. A play ends after the screen is set (the offense can shoot directly off the screen). From that point the play is reset and the offense begins again.

After five plays, switch sides.

To make the game easier:

- Play 2 v 3 or 3 v 4.
- Allow defenders to call out, "Switch!" and then switch players on screens.

To make the game more challenging:

- Require defenders to fight through or slide behind screens—no switching.

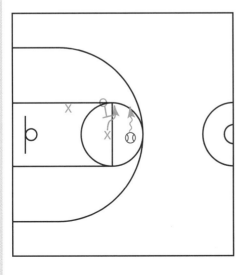

Figure 8.17 Defending against a screen.

Cutting Off Passing Lanes

The best defensive teams make it difficult for the offense to dribble and pass, much less shoot the ball. However, preventing passes is sometimes difficult.

The key to your players' denial of the opposition's passes is to have the off-ball defenders (those not guarding the ballhandler) maintain ball-player-self position (see figure 8.18). Help your players learn to use their peripheral vision so that they can see their players and the ball (without turning their heads) at all times. When the offense cuts toward the ball, good defenders try to beat them to the spot and cut them off from receiving the pass. Playing good team defense means trying to prevent your opponent from receiving the ball!

It's not easy; even pros have difficulty cutting off the passing lanes. Help your players adjust their positioning when their player is one or two passes away from the ball. They'll be a stronger defensive unit if they can understand this concept.

Figure 8.18   Ball-player-self position.

Cutting Off Passing Lanes Game

NO PASSING ZONE

Goal

To cut off passing lanes and intercept passes.

Description

Play 3 v 3. The defense tries to cut off the passing lanes and intercept the ball (see figure 8.19). Each player on offense can dribble no more than three times before passing. Offensive players move to open spaces to receive passes and then look to hit open teammates with passes.

The offense controls the ball for one minute. Then the teams switch sides. Within each one-minute period, the defense returns the ball to the offense if the defense steals it. Each steal counts for one point. Give each team five one-minute periods on defense.

To make the game easier:

○ Play 3 v 4.

○ Do not allow dribbling.

To make the game more challenging:

○ Play 4 v 3.

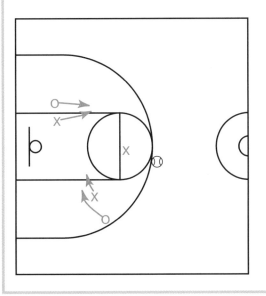

Figure 8.19 Cutting off a passing lane.

Helping Out

No matter how well your players position themselves and communicate on defense, an offensive player will at times spring free. Therefore, you must instruct your players on how to respond in these "help" situations.

Your instructions will vary depending on the type of help needed. For example, if one of your players spots an opponent wide open under the basket waving for a teammate to pass the ball, that defender should leave an assigned opponent who is farther from the basket and sprint to try to prevent the pass. On the other hand, if a dribbler gets by a defender and is headed for a layup, the defensive player closest to the dribbler between the dribbler and the basket should immediately move in to cut off the lane to the hoop (see figure 8.20). Whatever the case, the defender who has been beaten, or who loses an offensive player and sees that recovery is impossible, should shout, "Help!" All four teammates should be ready to respond if you have effectively taught them this very important defensive tactic.

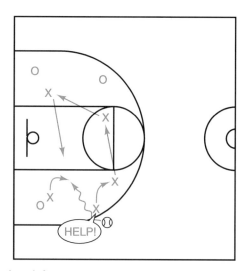

Figure 8.20 "Help" defense.

Helping Out Game

HELPING HANDS

Goal

To provide help when a teammate calls for it.

Description

Play 3 v 3. Tape off a 3-foot-by-3-foot area about 15 to 20 feet from the basket from any angle on the court (see figure 8.21). This area is the "freeze zone", i.e., when a defender enters that zone, he must freeze. Instruct the offense to dribble so that the player guarding the dribbler enters the freeze zone. When this happens, the dribbler should dribble toward the basket (the other offensive players should not be clustered around this freeze zone or in the dribbler's path), and the "frozen" defender should call, "Help!" The defender's teammates respond appropriately, trying to cut off the dribbler and defend against passes to the dribbler's teammates.

If the defense successfully provides help, it gets one point. *Note:* If help is not provided well, but the offense misses its shot, the defense does not get a point. Successful help means cutting off the dribbler and not allowing an easy scoring opportunity.

To make the game easier:

⊙ Play 3 v 4.

⊙ Make the freeze zone farther away from the basket.

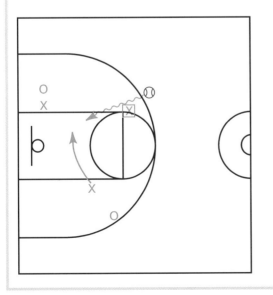

Figure 8.21   Providing help.

Individual Skills

This section describes the basketball skills you'll want your players to learn during the season. The skills are categorized as follows:

- Footwork
- Dribbling
- Passing and catching
- Shooting
- Rebounding
- Playing defense

Footwork

Good footwork is important to both offense and defense. Offensive players have the advantage over defenders in knowing what moves they will make and when. Offensive players use footwork to fake defenders off balance, move off screens, cut to the basket, prevent charging into a defender, and to elude a blockout when going for a rebound. Next we'll look at six types of footwork: slides, cuts, pivots, jump stops, jab steps, and drop steps.

Slides

A defender must be able to slide her feet and maintain an arm's distance from her opponent who is attempting to drive or cut to the basket. Younger players tend to cross their feet when attempting to move sideways. Instruct the player to stand in the ready position and then move the leg nearest her intended direction about two feet to that side. Next she should slide the other foot until the feet once again are shoulder-width apart (see figure 8.22a-b). She should use short, quick steps, with her weight evenly distributed on the balls of her feet. Remind the player to keep her toes pointed forward and to never cross her feet. She'll be able to slide more quickly if she keeps her knees bent, rear down, and back erect.

a   b

Figure 8.22   Lateral slide.

Figure 8.23   Crossing the feet during a lateral slide prevents a player from being able to move quickly.

Error Detection and Correction for Slides

ERROR   Players cross their feet, preventing themselves from changing direction or moving quickly (see figure 8.23).

CORRECTION   Instruct players to never cross their feet or not bring them closer together than shoulder-width apart.

Cuts

The ability to change direction quickly and in balance—to "cut"—is important on both the offensive and the defensive end of the court. Offensive players will have trouble getting open for passes or shots if they cannot "lose" their opponents with quick cuts. Defenders will find it difficult to keep up with effective offensive players if they are unable to respond to various cuts.

A player executes a cut by planting one foot on the court at the end of a slightly shortened stride, then pushing off that foot to shift his momentum in another direction. For example, a player pushes off with the left foot to cut to the right. Then he turns the unplanted foot in the direction he wants to go and leads with that leg as he bursts toward the new direction. When cutting, a player should bend his knees to lower his center of gravity and provide explosiveness from his legs. After cutting, he should get his lead hand up as a target for a pass.

Effective cuts are hard, sharp, and explosive. Three very effective cuts that offensive players use to get open are the L-cut, V-cut, and backdoor cut (see figure 8.24a-c). An offensive player should use an L- or V-cut when a defender has a foot and hand in the passing lane to deny the offensive player from catching the ball. In this case, the player should take the opponent to the basket, then sharply cut back to the outside. This is the most common way of getting open. A player should look to use a backdoor cut when a defender has a foot and hand in the passing lane to deny a pass from the outside. In this case, a player should move to the outside, then quickly cut behind his defender and toward the basket.

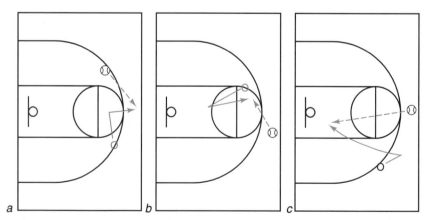

Figure 8.24   Cuts (a) L-cut, (b) V-cut, (c) backdoor cut.

Error Detection and Correction for Cuts

ERROR A player slows down with short steps before cutting and thus is not deceptive.

CORRECTION The player should focus on a two-count move: stepping first with the inside foot, using a slightly shortened step, and then with the outside foot, without crossing the feet.

ERROR A player circles on her cuts rather than making sharp cuts.

CORRECTION On the first step, the player should take a slightly shortened step, flex her knee to pivot sharply, and push off in the new direction. She should then shift her weight and take a long second step.

Pivots

Along with mastering the jump stop, learning to pivot correctly will give players a lot of confidence in their footwork. A pivot simply involves stopping, then turning on one foot to move forward (front pivot) or dropping one foot backward (back pivot), all while keeping the ball of one foot on the court (see figure 8.25a-b).

a   b

Figure 8.25 Proper technique for the pivot.

Remind players that after using a jump stop they may choose either foot as a pivot foot, but they may not change that pivot foot while in possession of the ball. When attempting a pass or shot, they may lift the designated pivot foot—providing they release the ball before the pivot foot again hits the floor. Each time they receive the ball, they should assume the ready position, and then they may use the pivot foot to

⊚ pivot to protect the ball from the defense,

⊚ pivot to pass to a teammate, or

⊚ pivot to make a move to the basket.

Error Detection and Correction for Pivoting

ERROR A player moves and switches the pivot foot while in possession of the ball.

CORRECTION Remind the player that once he chooses a pivot foot, he cannot lift that foot from the floor or slide it across the floor.

ERROR A player loses balance and lifts or drags the pivot foot.

CORRECTION The player should keep his weight on the ball of his pivot foot as he moves his nonpivot foot and maintains a balanced stance.

Jump Stops

One of the most common violations that younger players experience is traveling, usually because of poor stopping skills. You'll want to help your players learn how to start and stop with their bodies under control. They need to learn the jump stop so that they can stop after moving quickly either with or without the ball.

To practice the jump stop, players begin in the ready position, with arms relaxed and legs bent, feet shoulder-width apart, and weight shifted slightly forward to the balls of the feet (see figure 8.26).

Blow your whistle and have them sprint forward five or six steps. When they hear your whistle the second time, have them hop and stop quickly with both feet simultaneously hitting the floor, landing in a balanced and ready position.

By using the jump stop, a player is able to gather and control her forward momentum and may use either foot as a pivot foot for offensive moves. The jump stop is particularly advantageous when a player is moving under control without the ball, especially when she receives a pass while facing away from the basket in the low-post area (within eight feet of the basket).

Figure 8.26 Proper position for jump stop.

Error Detection and Correction for the Jump Stop

ERROR With his weight on his toes, a player loses balance, taking an extra step forward.

CORRECTION The player should shift his weight to the back of his feet, keeping the head up and over the waist.

Jab Steps

A jab step (also called a drive step) is a short (8 to 10 inches), quick step with the nonpivot foot straight toward the defender. The weight should be on the pivot foot, with the knees flexed and the upper body erect. A player uses a jab step to fake a drive and force her defender to react with a retreat step.

Drop Steps

The drop step, or reverse turn, is a basic pivoting move for pivoting backward. To perform a drop step, the player's back leads the way as he makes a reverse turn. The player should maintain a balanced stance, keep the weight on the ball of his pivot foot, and drop his nonpivot foot back (see figure 8.27a-b).

a   b

Figure 8.27　Proper technique for a drop step.

Footwork Game

TWO-STEPPIN'

Goal

To use pivots, drop steps, and jab steps to get free for shots.

Description

Play 3 v 3. When a player on the wing receives a pass, she does one of two things:

- Dribbles to the defender, stops, pivots, and shoots.
- Jabs or drop steps, then dribbles around a defender for a layup (see figure 8.28).

Award two points if the player performs the pivot, jab, or drop step correctly and gets a shot off; and an additional point for a made basket. Award one point for any made basket, whether made off of a pivot or jab or drop step.

To make the game easier:

- Play a "cold" defense (passive and about half speed).

To make the game more challenging:

- Award the two "performance" points only on made baskets.
- Don't award any points for baskets not made off of a pivot or jab or drop step.
- Play a "hot" (all-out) defense.

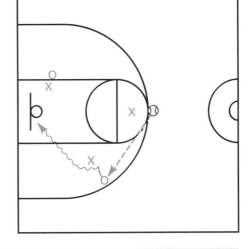

Figure 8.28   Using a jab or drop step to drive around a defender.

Dribbling

Dribbling is an integral part of basketball and vital to individual and team play. To maintain possession of the ball while moving, a player must dribble (tap or bounce the ball on the floor). At the start of the dribble the ball must leave the hand before the player lifts his pivot foot from the floor. The player may not touch the ball simultaneously with both hands while dribbling or allow it to come to a rest in his hand.

Dribbling is the most misused fundamental skill in the game. A pass travels much faster than a dribble, so before she dribbles, a player should look to pass to an open teammate. If a player dribbles too much, her teammates will tend not to move, making the defense's job easier. Excessive dribbling can destroy teamwork and morale. Dribbling should have a purpose: to take the player somewhere.

The three most common errors in dribbling are slapping at the ball from the chest area and waiting for it to bounce back up; keeping the head down, with eyes riveted to each bounce; and using one hand exclusively to bounce the ball. The ability to dribble with the weak hand as well as the strong hand is a key to advancing a player's ability level. If a player only dribbles with his strong hand, he can be overplayed to that side and made to be virtually ineffective.

As you correct these dribbling errors and attempt to improve your players' dribbling skills, advise them to

- establish a feel for the ball with the pads of the fingers;
- maintain the ready position, keeping knees bent and rear down;
- keep the dribble under control and always bounce the ball below waist height and even closer to the floor when being guarded closely;
- bounce the ball close to the body and protect the dribble from the defender with the nondribbling hand and arm;
- keep the head up and see the rest of the court (and teammates!);
- learn how to dribble with the right and left hand; and
- keep practicing!

Correct dribbling technique is shown in figure 8.29.

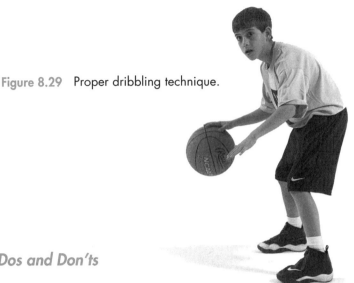

Figure 8.29 Proper dribbling technique.

Dribbling Dos and Don'ts

Dos

- Keep the dribble "alive" until you have a shot or an open teammate to pass to.
- Vary the speed and direction of the dribble so that defenders are kept off guard.
- Protect the dribble from the defensive player by using the nondribbling arm when being closely guarded.
- Cross over or switch dribbling hands to protect the ball after dribbling past the defender.
- Stay in the middle of the court and away from the sidelines and corners to avoid being trapped.

Don'ts

- Don't automatically start dribbling after receiving a pass. Look to see what shooting or passing options are available after squaring up to the basket.
- Don't pick up or stop dribbling with no other option (shot or pass) available.
- Don't dribble into a crowd—the ball is more likely to be stolen.
- Don't try to get fancy when good fundamental dribbling will do the job.
- Don't hesitate. Be assertive and confident when dribbling the ball.

There are many types and uses of dribbling. We'll look at three: the power dribble, the crossover dribble, and driving to the basket.

Power Dribble

A power dribble is a hard dribble that brings the ball up high and allows the player to get the ball high and make a move in a close space. It calls on many of the same fundamentals as described earlier for dribbling, combined with an explosive first step toward the basket or in whatever direction the player is dribbling.

The power dribble is most often used on a drive to the basket, but it can also be used to get out of a congested area (such as when rebounding and being surrounded by defenders with no open teammate to pass to). It's important that a player using a power dribble keep her head up and see the rim so that she can see open teammates and defenders. She should dribble off her finger pads with fingertip control, flexing the wrist and fingers to impart force to the ball without pumping the arm. Figure 8.30 below shows a power dribble.

Crossover Dribble

The crossover dribble is important in the open court on a fast break, to get open on a drive to the basket, and to create an opening for a shot. A player should use a crossover dribble when his defender overplays him on the ball side. The effectiveness of the crossover dribble depends on how sharply the dribbler changes direction of the dribble.

Figure 8.30 Power dribble.

To execute the crossover dribble, the player should cross the ball in front of her at a backward angle, switching the dribble from one hand to the other. She should keep the dribble close to her body and around knee level. As she makes the change of direction, she should get her nondribbling hand up and change her lead foot and body position for protection (see figure 8.31a-c).

a

b

c

Figure 8.31   Crossover dribble.

Error Detection and Correction for Dribbling

ERROR   A player looks at the ball when he's dribbling.

CORRECTION   Tell the player to keep his head up and see the rim.

ERROR   A player has trouble controlling the dribble.

CORRECTION   Instruct him to use his fingertips for control.

ERROR   A player doesn't protect the body while dribbling; he dribbles too high and far away from his body.

CORRECTION   Instruct him to protect the ball by keeping his nondribbling hand up and his body between the ball and the defender. He should dribble at knee level, close to his body.

Error Detection and Correction for the Crossover Dribble

ERROR   A player dribbles too high or wide as she changes direction.

CORRECTION   She should dribble at knee level and close to her body.

ERROR   A player does not protect the ball as she dribbles.

CORRECTION   She should protect the ball with her body and by keeping her nondribbling hand up.

Driving to the Basket

A ball handler with an opening to the basket should take a longer step past his defender's lead foot, take a long dribble with his outside hand (the hand farthest away from the defender), and drive while keeping his head up and his eyes on the basket (see figure 8.32a). He should drive in a straight line to the basket, close to his defender, cutting off his defender's retreat by closing the gap between himself and the defender's retreat step (see figure 8.32b). After driving by a defender, the player should be alert for defensive help and see the basket. He should finish by going in strong for a layup or passing to an open teammate who can score (see figure 8.32c).

a

b

c

Figure 8.32 Proper technique for driving to the basket.

Error Detection and Correction for Driving to the Basket

ERROR   A player makes her drive step too long, or she leans and puts weight on her drive-step foot (the right foot for a right-hander).

CORRECTION   She should keep her weight on their pivot foot as she executes the drive step. This enables her to move her lead foot quickly to shoot, pass, or drive.

Dribbling Games

IN MY DUST

Goal

To use power dribbles and crossover dribbles to attack the basket.

Description

Play 3 v 3 or 4 v 4 full court. Emphasize good fundamentals in all aspects, but place a special emphasis on effective dribbling by awarding one point each for made baskets, power dribbles, and crossover dribbles (see figure 8.33). Players should use these types of dribbles (leaving their opponents "in their dust") only as appropriate within the game; don't award points for ineffective or inappropriate use.

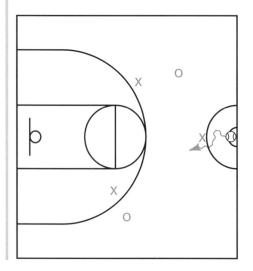

Figure 8.33 Using the crossover dribble to attack the basket.

DRIVE-THROUGH

Goal

To develop the ability to dribble under pressure.

Description

Play 3 v 3 or 4 v 4. Award the offense two points for scores off drives (see figure 8.34) and one point for other baskets.

To make the game easier:

⊙ Play a "cold" defense (passive and about half speed).

To make the game more challenging:

⊙ Play a "hot" (all-out) defense.

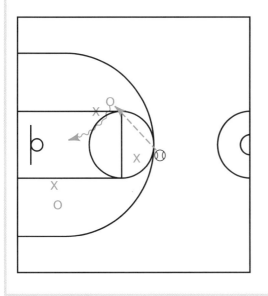

Figure 8.34   Driving to the basket.

Passing and Catching

Passing and catching are the keys to moving the ball effectively into position to take high-percentage shots. We'll address passing skills first.

Players pass the ball to maintain possession and create scoring opportunities. Passes should usually be short and crisp, because long or slow passes are likely to be stolen. However, players should avoid throwing too hard or using passes that are difficult to control. A player should pass the ball above the waist and within easy reach of the receiver. If possible, passes should be thrown to the receiver's side that is farthest from her defender. More skilled players can work on faking passes one way, then passing another.

Here we'll focus on three types of passes:

- chest pass
- bounce pass
- overhead pass

Chest Pass

Chest passes can be used quickly and accurately from most positions on the floor. The chest pass is so named because the ball is thrown with two hands from the passer's chest to the receiver's chest area. A player should begin in the ready position and step toward his target to initiate the pass (see figure 8.35a). While all players need to see their targets, more advanced players should practice seeing their targets without looking at them by looking or faking away before passing. A player should step in the direction of the target, extending her legs, back, and arms. Emphasize forcing the weak hand through the ball; the strong hand tends to dominate (see figure 8.35b). Releasing it off the first and second fingers of both hands gives the ball backspin and direction. A player should follow through with his fingers pointed at the target, palms facing down (see figure 8.35c).

Figure 8.35 Proper technique for a chest pass.

Error Detection and Correction for the Chest Pass

ERROR   A player's chest passes lack force.

CORRECTION   Have the player start her passes with her elbows in and force her wrists and fingers through the ball.

ERROR   A player's chest passes are not accurate.

CORRECTION   She should point her fingers at the target. The pass will go where her fingers direct it.

Bounce Pass

Sometimes it is easier for a passer to get the ball to a teammate by bouncing the ball once on the court before it reaches the receiver. For example, a defender may be guarding a player with both hands overhead, preventing a pass through the air to a teammate. In that case a bounce pass may be the only route to get the ball to a teammate. Players should use bounce passes when they are closely guarded and may not have the space to extend their arms in a chest pass.

Teach players to bounce the ball on the court two-thirds of the way between themselves and the receivers, as illustrated in figure 8.36. Remind them to use their legs and to step toward their targets. Snapping the thumbs down and together as the passer releases the pass gives the ball some backspin. Backspin slows the pass down a little as it hits the floor and gives the receiver a chance to catch the ball at waist level in ready position.

Figure 8.36   Proper technique for a bounce pass.

Error Detection and Correction for the Bounce Pass

ERROR   Bounce passes are too high and too slow.

CORRECTION   The player should start the pass from waist level and aim the ball's bounce closer to the receiver.

ERROR   Bounce passes are too low.

CORRECTION   Start the pass from waist level and aim it to bounce farther from the target so that the receiver can catch the ball at waist level.

Overhead Pass

Players use an overhead pass when they are closely guarded and have to pass over their defender—for instance, an outlet pass to start a fast break, or a lob pass to a player cutting backdoor to the basket. The overhead pass is also an option for feeding the low post. The player should start in a balanced stance, holding the ball above his forehead with elbows in and flexed at about 90 degrees (see figure 8.37a). The player should not bring the ball behind his head, because it takes longer to make the pass and the ball is easier to steal in that position. Direct the player to step in the direction of the target and extend his legs and back. He should quickly pass the ball, extending his arms and flexing his wrists and fingers, releasing the ball off the first and second fingers of both hands (see figure 8.37b). The player follows through ends with fingers pointing at the target, palms facing down.

a

b

Figure 8.37   Proper technique for overhead pass.

Error Detection and Correction for the Overhead Pass

ERROR   Overhead passes lack force.

CORRECTION   Make sure the player doesn't bring the ball behind her head, because this tends to force her elbows out, leading to an incomplete follow-through. She should not break the plane of her body. Force comes from keeping the elbows in, flexing wrists and fingers, and extending legs, back, and arms.

Passing Game

PASSING FAD

Goal

To set up good shots through passing.

Description

Play 3 v 2 or 4 v 3. Award the offense one point for each successful pass and one point for a basket (see figure 8.38).

Occasionally vary the game by asking players to use only a certain type of pass: chest, bounce, or overhead (or slant the game by awarding more points for a particular type of pass).

To make the game easier:

⊙ Play 3 v 1 or 4 v 2.

To make the game more challenging:

⊙ Play 3 v 3 or 3 v 4.

⊙ Allow no dribbling.

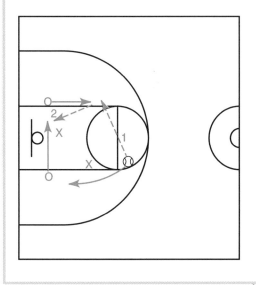

Figure 8.38   Passing to set up shots.

Catching

Even the best passes are of little value if they aren't caught. Sloppy receiving technique is often the cause of turnovers and missed scoring opportunities. Emphasize the following receiving techniques:

1. Show a target to the passer by putting an arm up or out to the side and call for the ball (see figure 8.39).
2. Move to meet the pass—step toward the ball, not away.
3. Watch the ball come into the hands (see figure 8.40).
4. Use two hands, palms facing the passer, thumbs together.

Figure 8.39 The receiver of a pass should put up a hand to give the passer a target.

Figure 8.40 Proper technique for catching a pass.

When possible, a player should come to a jump stop after receiving a pass with his feet positioned shoulder-width apart in ready position. From this position, the player should pivot to face the basket, looking for an open teammate, a shot, or a lane to dribble the ball to the basket.

Error Detection and Correction for Catching

ERROR   A player fumbles passes.

CORRECTION   Instruct the player to keep her hands up and see the ball all the way into her hands. She should keep her hands relaxed and give with the ball as she catches it.

Triple Threat Position

The triple threat position is a version of the ready position: the player holds the ball to the side on the hip with elbows out (see figure 8.41). This position gives the player the options of shooting, passing, or dribbling. Such a position makes the defender uncertain of what the ballhandler will do, and it gives the ballhandler a number of choices.

To keep a defender off guard, a player in the triple threat position should move the ball between shooting, passing, and driving positions, keeping the ball close to the chest and never lower than the waist. The player's hands should remain in shooting position; a player must be a threat to shoot before the options of passing or driving become viable.

Figure 8.41   The triple threat position.

Error Detection and Correction for the Triple Threat Position

ERROR A player faces to the left or right, limiting his moves with the ball in that direction.

CORRECTION Instruct him to square up to the basket with his body facing the basket and the defender, in a good position to shoot, pass, or drive to the right or the left.

ERROR A player lowers the ball, limiting his moves to a drive, or he raises the ball above his head, limiting his moves to an overhead pass.

CORRECTION The player should keep the ball moving close to his chest so that he is a triple threat to shoot, pass, or drive.

Shooting

Every player loves to put the basketball through the hoop. So your players will be highly motivated to learn proper shooting technique if you convince them that it will help them make more of their shots.

To instill the fundamentals of shooting and encourage your players to learn them, tell them they'll SCORE if they do these things:

S – Select only high-percentage shots (shots that are likely to go in).

C – Concentrate on the target.

O – Order movements: square up, bend knees and elbows, cock wrist.

R – Release and wave "good-bye" to the ball (have the shooting hand follow through).

E – Extend the shooting arm up and out toward the basket.

Players can shoot the ball in a variety of ways, including set and jump shots, free throws, layups, and shooting off a dribble.

Set and Jump Shots

Although the most common shot at higher levels of play is the jump shot, young players who lack the leg strength and coordination to spring from the floor while shooting will more often shoot set shots. Teach younger players the mechanics of the set shot first, and they will be able to advance to the jump shot as they increase their strength and improve their coordination.

Teach your players these shooting mechanics in this sequence:

1. Lay the ball on the finger pads of each hand, with the shooting hand behind and slightly underneath the ball and the nonshooting hand balancing the ball from the side.

2. Focus on a specific target, usually the rim or backboard. The middle of the rim should be the target for most shots, but when you're at a 30- to 60-degree angle from the hoop, sight the corner of the square on the backboard for a bank shot (see figure 8.42a).

3. Align shoulders, hips, and feet square with (facing) the basket. The foot on the shooting-hand side can be up to six inches in front of the other foot so that the base of support is comfortable and balanced.

4. Bend the knees to get momentum for the shot. Let the legs, not the arms, be the primary power source for the shot.

5. Bend the shooting-arm elbow to approximately a 90-degree angle, keeping the forearm perpendicular to the floor and in front of the cocked wrist as the ball is brought up to the shooting position above the forehead (see figure 8.42b).

6. As you extend the legs, release the ball by extending the elbow, bringing the wrist forward, and moving the fingers of the shooting hand up and through the ball (see figure 8.42c). The nonshooting arm and hand should maintain their supportive position on the side of the ball until after the release.

7. Follow through after the release by landing on both feet, extending the shooting arm and dropping the wrist, pointing the index finger of the shooting hand directly at the basket.

a (continued)

Figure 8.42 Proper technique for a set shot.

Figure 8.42   *(continued)*

b

c

Check that your players aren't shooting "line drives" at the hoop. Help them to see how important proper arch is in allowing the shot a reasonable chance to go in. Remind them to shoot the ball up, then out, toward the basket.

A jump shot is similar to shooting a set shot except for two adjustments:

1. You align the ball higher and shoot after jumping, rather than shooting with the simultaneous extension of your legs.
2. Because you jump first and then shoot, your upper body, arm, wrist, and fingers must generate more force.

The player should jump straight up off both feet, fully extending the ankles, knees, back, and shoulders (see figure 8.43). The height of the jump depends on the range of the shot. On shots close to the basket when the player is closely guarded, he will have to jump higher than his defenders. On longer-range jump shots, he will usually have more

Figure 8.43 Proper technique for a jump shot.

time and defenders are not quite as close. Therefore, the player doesn't have to jump as high for long-range shots. More force from the legs can be used for shooting the ball rather than for jumping high. Balance and control are more important than gaining maximum height on a jump. Smooth rhythm and complete follow-through are also important.

Error Detection and Correction for Shooting Set and Jump Shots

ERROR Shots are short.

CORRECTION The player should generate more force from her legs. She may also need to speed up her rhythm or make it more even-paced.

ERROR Shots are long.

CORRECTION The player needs to put more arc into the ball. Her shoulders should be relaxed and in a forward position; she should move her hands closer together if they are too far apart; and she should raise her shooting arm higher to provide more arc.

ERROR Shots hit the sides of the rim.

CORRECTION The player should square up to the basket, setting the ball on the shooting side of her head between her ear and shoulder with her elbow in. Her shooting arm, wrist, and fingers should go straight toward the basket.

Shooting Game

BUCKETMANIA

Goal

To score as many baskets as possible.

Description

Play 3 v 2. Give the three players on offense five minutes to score as many baskets as possible against the defense (see figure 8.44). After

(continued)

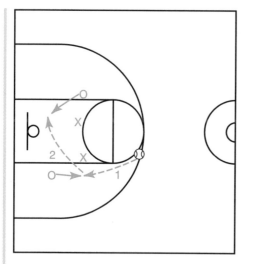

Bucketmania, *(continued)*

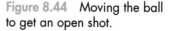
Figure 8.44   Moving the ball to get an open shot.

each made basket and defensive rebound, the ball is returned to the offense. After five minutes, switch the offense and defense, keeping one of the offensive players on offense so that it remains 3 v 2. Give the new offense five minutes to score as many baskets as possible. Compare the teams' totals.

Adapt this game to focus on different types of shots, if you want. Either call for only a certain type of shot (e.g., jump shot, layup, shot off a dribble), or award more points for baskets from one of those shots to emphasize that shot.

To make the game easier:

⊙ Play 3 v 1 or 4 v 2.

⊙ Play a "cold" defense (half speed, passive).

To make the game more challenging:

⊙ Play 3 v 3 or 4 v 4.

⊙ Play a "hot" defense (all out).

Free Throws

Success in free-throw shooting requires sound mechanics, a routine, relaxation, rhythm, concentration, and confidence. Routine, relaxation, and rhythm contribute to concentration and confidence.

A routine helps players relax, focus, and shoot with confidence and rhythm. A routine can include dribbling a set number, checking mechanics, using visualization to practice mentally shooting the free throw just before shooting it, and taking a deep breath to relax (see figure 8.45). The same form as described for the set shot should be used for free throws.

Figure 8.45 Having a routine before a free throw helps a player relax, focus, and shoot with confidence.

Error Detection and Correction for Shooting Free Throws

ERROR   A player feels tense when shooting free throws.

CORRECTION   Instruct her to breathe in deeply and exhale fully and to relax her shoulders, arms, hands, and fingers, letting them drop and loosen. She should focus on positive thoughts, such as, "I'm a good shooter," and visualize the ball going through the basket.

Free-Throw Shooting Game

ON THE LINE

Goal

To make free throws in game-winning situations.

Description

Split your squad into two even teams. The regulation "game" has ended in a tie score. It will be decided by free throws. Each player

(continued)

On the Line *(continued)*

shoots two free throws: first a player from team A, then one from team B (see figure 8.46). Each team can determine its own shooting order. Continue in this fashion until all players have shot their two free throws, and total the points to determine the winner. If the game is still tied, keep the same order of players and have a "sudden-death" shoot-off, with the first player from team A shooting one free throw, followed by the first player from team B. The first time the tie is broken after a player from team B has shot in this shoot-off, the game is over.

To make the game easier:

⊙ Move the free-throw line up a few feet.

To make the game more challenging:

⊙ Require the winning team to make at least four consecutive free throws in addition to making more free throws than its opponent.

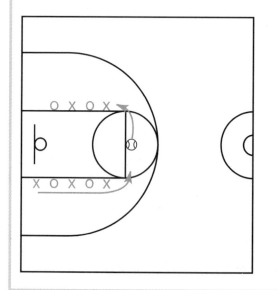

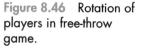

Figure 8.46 Rotation of players in free-throw game.

Layups

The highest-percentage shot, and therefore the most desirable shot, is a layup. A layup is a one-handed shot taken within three feet of the basket (see figure 8.47). Teach players to use their left hands when shooting layups from the left side of the basket and their right hands when shooting from the right side of the basket. The layup motion begins with the player striding from a 45- to 60-degree angle to the hoop and planting and exploding—much like a high jumper—off the foot opposite the shooting hand. The player explodes off the planted foot straight up into the air. At the top of the jump, the player releases the ball by bringing the shooting hand, which is underneath the ball and near the shoulder, up toward the basket. As in the set shot, the index finger of the shooting hand should be pointed directly at the basket or the appropriate spot on the backboard.

Your right-handed players are likely to find left-handed layups troublesome, just as your left-handed players are going to find right-handed layups difficult. Point out to them the reason for using the hand farthest from the basket to shoot the ball: The ball is more easily protected.

Figure 8.47   Proper technique for a layup.

Error Detection and Correction for Shooting Layups

ERROR A player swivels the ball to the side before shooting, allowing it to be blocked or stolen.

CORRECTION Instruct the player to lift the ball straight up as he shoots.

ERROR The ball hits low on the backboard and, with slight contact on the arm, falls short.

CORRECTION The player should shoot high off the backboard so that the ball drops in the basket. This way, even if the player is fouled on the shot, the ball will have a chance to go in.

Shooting Off a Dribble

When shooting off a dribble, the player should pick up the ball while facing the basket in position to shoot. She shouldn't reach for the ball but should pick it up in front of her shooting knee with the knees flexed to gain balance for the shot.

When a player is dribbling to his strong-hand side, he should jump behind his last dribble and pick the ball up in front of his shooting knee. When a player is dribbling to his weak-hand side, he should use a crossover dribble on his last dribble to pick the ball up in front of his shooting knee.

Error Detection and Correction for Shooting Off a Dribble

ERROR A player floats forward, backward, or to a side when shooting.

CORRECTION Have the player pick the ball up in front of her shooting knee with her knees flexed to gain balance for the shot.

Rebounding

Possession of the ball comes more often from missed shots than any other way. The team that controls the backboards usually controls the game. Offensive rebounding adds to your team's chances to score, and defensive rebounding limits your opponent's scoring opportunities.

More than any other basketball skill, rebounding relies on a player's desire and courage. Good rebounders are able to anticipate missed shots and determine how hard or how soft, or to what side of the rim, the ball will rebound. They also know where their opponents are at all times, and they are able to "box out" their opposing player by getting between the opposing player and the basket and putting their rears in contact with the opponents (see figure 8.48).

A player may use a front or rear pivot to turn and box out his opponent. A front pivot allows the defense to turn while watching the offense move toward the rebound. A rear pivot is used to move into the path of the offense without the same visual contact. Encourage defenders to use whichever method gets them in position in front of the offense, sealing the offensive player away from the basket.

Figure 8.48   Boxing out.

A player should avoid reaching over an opponent when she gets boxed out; she'll get called for a foul if she does. Emphasize the importance of jumping straight up for the rebound. By jumping vertically, not only will a player achieve great height, but she'll also avoid needless fouls.

Here are some additional rebounding tips to share with your players:

⊙ A shot taken from the side is likely to rebound to the opposite side of the basket. Therefore, players should try to get positioned on the opposite side of the basket when such a shot is taken.

⊙ Once contact is established with an opposing player, the defensive rebounder wants to maintain that contact until releasing to jump for the rebound.

⊙ After controlling a rebound, a player should keep the ball at chin level with her elbows out (see figure 8.49).

Use the following guidelines in coaching your players to rebound free throws:

⊙ Have your best rebounders in the positions closest to the basket.

⊙ Remind players to block out the players next to them when the opposing team is shooting.

⊙ Designate a player to block out the shooter when the opposing team is shooting.

⊙ Have one player near midcourt to prevent easy fast breaks by the opponents when your team is shooting.

Figure 8.49 Proper position after controlling a rebound.

Error Detection and Correction for Rebounding

ERROR Your players watch the ball, and their opponents gain position for the rebound.

CORRECTION Instruct players to locate their opponents first, get inside position, block out, and then go for the ball.

ERROR Players have trouble holding onto rebounds.

CORRECTION They need to catch rebounds firmly with two hands.

ERROR After gaining rebounds, a player has the ball stripped by an opponent.

CORRECTION The player must protect the ball, keeping it above her forehead with her elbows out and away from her opponent.

Rebounding Game

CLEANING THE GLASS

Goal

To get the rebound.

Description

Play 2 v 2, with the coach as a nonplaying shooter. Each play begins with the coach shooting at the basket, intentionally missing the shot (see figure 8.50). The two players on offense try to rebound and score, and the defense also tries to rebound. If the offense makes a basket or the defense gets the ball, the play is over. Give the offense five straight plays, and then switch offense and defense. Each rebound is worth one point, as is each basket. Keep track of points and compare them at the end.

(continued)

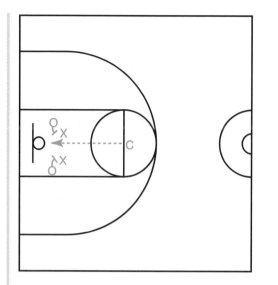

Figure 8.50　In position to rebound.

Playing Defense

Individual defensive skills are sometimes less appreciated than individual offensive techniques, but they are just as important. Your players need to learn the basics of player-to-player defense, both on the ball and off the ball, to compete successfully.

On the Ball

Defenders can best keep their opponents (the players with the ball) from scoring by staying between the opponents and the basket. Defenders should try to maintain an arm's distance from the offensive player with the ball.

Tell your players to consider these things about their bodies and court positions when guarding a player with the ball:

Body position

⊙ Am I in ready position and alert?

⊙ Am I arm's distance from my player (the ballhandler) and able to put pressure on his ability to shoot, pass, or drive?

Court position

⊙ Is my player close enough to attempt a good shot?

⊙ Am I close enough to the player to prevent an easy shot?

⊙ Am I too close, so the opponent can drive around me?

⊙ Will a teammate be able to help me if the player beats me with the dribble?

Have your players focus on the opponent's midsection (see figure 8.51a). If defenders watch the ball or their opponent's head or feet, the defenders are likely to react to a fake that will put them out of position. As the offensive player begins to dribble, the defender should react by sliding the feet and maintaining an arm's distance from the opponent, trying to beat the offensive player to the spot that the player wants to reach (see figure 8.51b). If the defender can get the offensive player to stop and pick up the ball, the defender can then move closer and crowd the offensive player by blocking the passing lanes, applying extensive pressure with the arms (see figure 8.51c).

a

b   c

Figure 8.51   Proper technique for defending a player with the ball.

More advanced defenders can focus on four defensive strategies when playing defense on the ball:

1. **Turning the dribbler.** Defenders who establish position a half body ahead of the dribbler can force the dribbler to turn or reverse direction.

2. **Forcing the dribbler to the sideline.** When a defensive player forces the dribbler to dribble toward the sideline, the dribbler can pass in only one direction. A defender can do this by working for position a half body to the inside of the court, with the inside foot (the one closer to the middle of the court) forward and the outside foot back.

3. **Funneling the dribbler to the middle.** By taking position a half body to the outside of the court, a defender can force a dribbler to the middle. This strategy will move the dribbler toward one of the defender's teammates off the ball.

4. **Forcing the dribbler to use the weak hand.** By overplaying the strong hand, defenders can force the dribbler to use the weak hand. Defenders can overplay the strong hand by being a half body to the dribbler's strong-hand side.

On the Ball Defense Game

PICKIN' POCKETS

Goal

To steal the ball or otherwise create turnovers.

Description

Play 3 v 4 or 2 v 3. The offense must complete four passes before shooting. The object is for the defense to use their defensive positioning to force a turnover or steal (see figure 8.52). The defense is on defense for two minutes; then switch offense and defense. Award two points to the defense for each turnover. As an option, you might also want to award a single point for any of these actions:

◎ Forcing a dribbler to a sideline

◎ Funneling a dribbler to the middle (assuming defensive teammates are in the middle to help out)

◎ Forcing a dribbler to use the weak hand

To make the game easier:
  ⊙ Play 3 v 5 or 2 v 4.

To make the game more challenging:
  ⊙ Play 3 v 3 or 4 v 4.

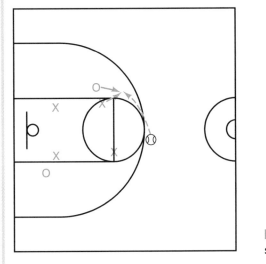

Figure 8.52   Going for the steal.

Off the Ball

Defending an opponent without the ball is just as important as guarding a player with the ball, but it is a bit more complicated. Whether an opponent is one pass or two passes away from the ball, defensive players need to apply the defensive concept of ball-player-self (see figure 8.53). Defenders should position themselves so that they can see the ball (and know if they need to come and help a teammate on a pass or drive), and they must keep track of a moving opponent (their player), who may be trying to get open to receive a pass. The closer an opponent is to the ball, the closer the defender should be to that opponent. The farther the ball is from an opponent, the farther away a defender can play that opponent and be able to give help to the teammate guarding the ball.

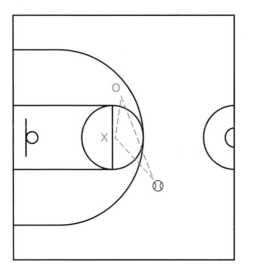

Figure 8.53　Proper position for defending a player off the ball.

Error Detection and Correction for Guarding Off the Ball

ERROR　Defenders off the ball lose track of their offensive player.

CORRECTION　Position players to see the ball and their player without turning their head. They should establish and maintain the ball-player-self relationship. Have the player point at the ball with one hand and at his player with the other. The player must adjust position as the offensive player or ball changes position. A player two or more passes away needs to be alert to help out on a drive or deflect a long pass attempt to his opponent in the corner (see figure 8.54).

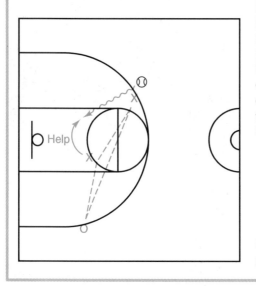

Figure 8.54　Proper ball-player-self positioning.

Denial Position. A player should use the denial position when her opponent is one pass away from the ball. The space between two offensive players where a pass can be made is called the passing lane. A defender wants to have an arm and leg in the passing lane when guarding a player who is one pass away (see figure 8.55). This denial position allows the defender to establish the ball-player-self relationship and discourages the offensive player with the ball from attempting a pass.

Open Position. When offensive players are two or more passes away from the ball, the defensive player wants to establish an open position that still maintains the ball-player-self relationship. In the open position the defender is farther away from the offensive player, pointing to the ball with one hand and the opponent with the other hand (see figure 8.56). Using peripheral vision, the defender moves to react as the ball penetrates toward the basket (to help out on the drive) or into denial position if the offensive player cuts hard to receive a pass. In both the denial and open positions, the key is remembering always to maintain the ball-player-self relationship.

Figure 8.55 Denial position.

Figure 8.56 Open position.

Season Plans

Hopefully you've learned a lot from this book: what your responsibilities as a coach are, how to communicate well and provide for safety, how to use the games approach to teach and shape skills, and how to coach on game days. But game days make up only a portion of your season—you and your players will spend more time in practice than in competition. How well you conduct practices and prepare your players for competition will greatly affect both your and your players' enjoyment and success throughout the season.

In this chapter, then, we present three season plans: one for 8- to 9-year-olds, one for 10- to 11-year-olds, and one for 12- to 14-year-olds. Use these plans as guidelines for conducting your practices. These plans are not the *only* way to approach your season, but they do present an appropriate teaching progression. Remember to incorporate the games approach as you use these plans, using Game 1 to put your players in a game-like situation that introduces them to the main tactic or skill that you want them to learn that day. Then guide your players through a short question-and-answer session that leads to the skill practice. Here you should conduct one or two skill practices in which you will teach players the tactic or skill and then conduct a fun drill for them to practice that skill.

Refer to chapter 5 (page 47) for how to run a practice. In chapter 8 you will find descriptions of all the tactics and skills, and games you can use to practice them. Throughout the season plans we refer you to the appropriate pages for those tactics and skills and games.

Remember to keep the introductions, demonstrations, and explanations of the tactics and skills brief. As the players practice, attend to individual players, guiding them with tips or with further demonstration.

Good luck and good coaching!

Season Plan for 8- to 9-Year-Olds

Many 8- to 9-year-olds have had little or no exposure to basketball. Don't assume they have any knowledge of the game. Help them explore the basic tactics and skills of the sport, as suggested in the following season plan.

Practice 1

- **Purpose:** To understand the basic concepts of the game
- **Warm-up**
- **Game 1:** Scrimmage
- **Skill Practice:** Demonstrate positions, basic concepts of offense and defense (see pages 76 and 91)
- **Game 2:** Scrimmage
- **Cool-down and Review**

Practice 2

- **Purpose:** To learn passing techniques
- **Warm-up**
- **Game 1:** Passing Fad (see page 121)
- **Skill Practice:** Passing (see page 116)

○ **Game 2:** Passing Fad

○ **Cool-down and Review**

Practice 3

○ **Purpose:** To learn dribbling techniques

○ **Warm-up**

○ **Game 1:** Drive-Through (see page 115)

○ **Skill Practice:** Dribbling (see page 108)

○ **Game 2:** Drive-Through or In My Dust (see page 114)

○ **Cool-down and Review**

Practice 4

○ **Purpose:** To learn proper shooting technique

○ **Warm-up**

○ **Game 1:** Bucketmania (see page 129)

○ **Skill Practice:** Shooting (see page 124)

○ **Game 2:** Bucketmania

○ **Cool-down and Review**

Practice 5

○ **Purpose:** To shoot free throws effectively

○ **Warm-up**

○ **Game 1:** On the Line (see page 131)

○ **Skill Practice:** Shooting free throws (see page 130)

○ **Game 2:** On the Line

○ **Cool-down and Review**

Practice 6

○ **Purpose:** To learn proper footwork

○ **Warm-up**

○ **Game 1:** Two-Steppin' (see page 107)

○ **Skill Practice:** Pivots, drop steps, and jab steps (see page 103-106)

○ **Game 2:** Two-Steppin'

○ **Cool-down and Review**

Practice 7

- ⊙ **Purpose:** To learn proper rebounding technique
- ⊙ **Warm-up**
- ⊙ **Game 1:** Cleaning the Glass (see page 137)
- ⊙ **Skill Practice:** Rebounding (see page 134)
- ⊙ **Game 2:** Cleaning the Glass
- ⊙ **Cool-down and Review**

Practice 8

- ⊙ **Purpose:** To learn how to create passing lanes
- ⊙ **Warm-up**
- ⊙ **Game 1:** Room to Move (see page 77)
- ⊙ **Skill Practice:** Creating passing lanes (see page 78)
- ⊙ **Game 2:** Room to Move
- ⊙ **Cool-down and Review**

Practice 9

- ⊙ **Purpose:** To learn how to cut off passing lanes
- ⊙ **Warm-up**
- ⊙ **Game 1:** No Passing Zone (see page 97)
- ⊙ **Skill Practice:** Cutting off passing lanes (see page 96)
- ⊙ **Game 2:** No Passing Zone
- ⊙ **Cool-down and Review**

Practice 10

- ⊙ **Purpose:** To attack the basket by using the give-and-go play
- ⊙ **Warm-up**
- ⊙ **Game 1:** Return to Sender (see page 85)
- ⊙ **Skill Practice:** Give-and-go play (see page 83)
- ⊙ **Game 2:** Return to Sender
- ⊙ **Cool-down and Review**

Practice 11

- ⊙ **Purpose:** To win the ball by playing tight defense
- ⊙ **Warm-up**
- ⊙ **Game 1:** Helping Hands (see page 99)

- **Skill Practice:** Cutting off passing lanes (see page 96) and helping out (see page 98)
- **Game 2:** Helping Hands or No Passing Zone (see page 97-99)
- **Cool-down and Review**

Practice 12

- **Purpose:** To practice proper rebounding technique
- **Warm-up**
- **Game 1:** Cleaning the Glass (see page 137)
- **Skill Practice:** Rebounding (see page 134)
- **Game 2:** Cleaning the Glass
- **Cool-down and Review**

Practice 13

- **Purpose:** To practice playing effective team offense
- **Warm-up**
- **Game 1:** Return to Sender (see page 85)
- **Skill Practice:** Give-and-go (see page 85), creating passing lanes (see page 78)
- **Game 2:** Return to Sender (see page 85) or Room to Move (see page 77)
- **Cool-down and Review**

Practice 14

- **Purpose:** To practice playing effective team defense
- **Warm-up**
- **Game 1:** Helping Hands (see page 99)
- **Skill Practice:** Cutting off passing lanes (see page 96) and helping out (see page 98)
- **Game 2:** Helping Hands or No Passing Zone (see page 97-99)
- **Cool-down and Review**

Season Plan for 10- to 11-Year-Olds

This season plan builds upon the previous one as players practice the fundamental tactics and skills and add a few new tactics, including setting screens (and defending against screens), executing the pick-and-roll, shooting jump shots, and doing a crossover dribble.

Practice 1

- **Purpose:** To attack the basket through passing and dribbling
- **Warm-up**
- **Game 1:** Passing Fad (see page 121)
- **Skill Practice:** Bounce, chest, and overhead passing (see pages 116-121), dribbling (see page 116-120)
- **Game 2:** Drive-Through (see page 115)
- **Cool-down and Review**

Practice 2

- **Purpose:** To learn proper footwork
- **Warm-up**
- **Game 1:** Two-Steppin' (see page 107)
- **Skill Practice:** Slides, cuts, pivots, jump stops, drop steps, jab steps (see page 100-106)
- **Game 2:** Two-Steppin'
- **Cool-down and Review**

Practice 3

- **Purpose:** To learn proper shooting technique
- **Warm-up**
- **Game 1:** Bucketmania (see page 129)
- **Skill Practice:** Shooting (see page 124)
- **Game 2:** Bucketmania
- **Cool-down and Review**

Practice 4

- **Purpose:** To shoot free throws effectively
- **Warm-up**
- **Game 1:** On the Line (see page 131)
- **Skill Practice:** Shooting free throws (see page 130)
- **Game 2:** On the Line
- **Cool-down and Review**

Practice 5

- **Purpose:** To learn to set screens and execute pick-and-rolls
- **Warm-up**

- **Game 1:** Screen Door (see page 79)
- **Skill Practice:** Setting screens (see page 79), pick-and-roll (see page 86)
- **Game 2:** Pickin' for Points (see page 87)
- **Cool-down and Review**

Practice 6

- **Purpose:** To learn to defend against screens and pick-and-rolls
- **Warm-up**
- **Game 1:** Cut Off at the Pass (see page 95)
- **Skill Practice:** Defending against screens (see page 95)
- **Game 2:** Helping Hands (see page 99)
- **Cool-down and Review**

Practice 7

- **Purpose:** To learn to use the crossover dribble in attacking the basket
- **Warm-up**
- **Game 1:** In My Dust (see page 114)
- **Skill Practice:** Cross-over dribble (see page 111)
- **Game 2:** In My Dust
- **Cool-down and Review**

Practice 8

- **Purpose:** To practice proper rebounding technique
- **Warm-up**
- **Game 1:** Cleaning the Glass (see page 137)
- **Skill Practice:** Rebounding (see page 134)
- **Game 2:** Cleaning the Glass
- **Cool-down and Review**

Practice 9

- **Purpose:** To learn how to create passing lanes
- **Warm-up**
- **Game 1:** Room to Move (see page 77)
- **Skill Practice:** Creating passing lanes (see page 78)
- **Game 2:** Room to Move
- **Cool-down and Review**

Practice 10

⊙ **Purpose:** To learn how to cut off passing lanes
⊙ **Warm-up**
⊙ **Game 1:** No Passing Zone (see page 97)
⊙ **Skill Practice:** Cutting off passing lanes (see page 96) and helping out (see page 98)
⊙ **Game 2:** Helping Hands (see page 99)
⊙ **Cool-down and Review**

Practice 11

⊙ **Purpose:** To practice playing effective team offense
⊙ **Warm-up**
⊙ **Game 1:** Return to Sender (see page 85)
⊙ **Skill Practice:** Give-and-go (see page 85), creating passing lanes (see page 78)
⊙ **Game 2:** Return to Sender (see page 85) or Room to Move (see page 77)
⊙ **Cool-down and Review**

Practice 12

⊙ **Purpose:** To practice playing effective team defense
⊙ **Warm-up**
⊙ **Game 1:** Pickin' Pockets (see page 140)
⊙ **Skill Practice:** Cutting off passing lanes (see page 96), helping out (see page 98), playing on the ball and off the ball defense (see page 138)
⊙ **Game 2:** Pickin' Pockets or Helping Hands (see page 99) or No Passing Zone (see page 97)
⊙ **Cool-down and Review**

Practice 13

⊙ **Purpose:** To learn to set screens and execute pick-and-rolls
⊙ **Warm-up**
⊙ **Game 1:** Screen Door (see page 79)
⊙ **Skill Practice:** Setting screens (see page 79), pick-and-roll (see page 87)
⊙ **Game 2:** Pickin' for Points (see page 87)
⊙ **Cool-down and Review**

Practice 14

- ⊙ **Purpose:** To learn to defend against screens and pick-and-rolls
- ⊙ **Warm-up**
- ⊙ **Game 1:** Cut Off at the Pass (see page 95)
- ⊙ **Skill Practice:** Defending against screens (see page 95)
- ⊙ **Game 2:** Helping Hands (see page 99)
- ⊙ **Cool-down and Review**

Season Plan for 12- to 14-Year-Olds

At this stage players are refining the skills they have learned from past years. This season plan builds upon the previous one and adds a few new tactics, including the transition game and the power dribble.

Practice 1

- ⊙ **Purpose:** To attack the basket through passing and dribbling
- ⊙ **Warm-up**
- ⊙ **Game 1:** Passing Fad (see page 121)
- ⊙ **Skill Practice:** Bounce, chest, and overhead passing (see page 116-120), dribbling and crossover dribbling (see page 110)
- ⊙ **Game 2:** In My Dust (see page 114)
- ⊙ **Cool-down and Review**

Practice 2

- ⊙ **Purpose:** To learn proper footwork
- ⊙ **Warm-up**
- ⊙ **Game 1:** Two-Steppin' (see page 107)
- ⊙ **Skill Practice:** Slides, cuts, pivots, jump stops, drop steps, jab steps (see page 100-106)
- ⊙ **Game 2:** Two-Steppin'
- ⊙ **Cool-down and Review**

Practice 3

- ⊙ **Purpose:** To learn proper shooting technique
- ⊙ **Warm-up**
- ⊙ **Game 1:** Bucketmania (see page 129)
- ⊙ **Skill Practice:** Shooting (see page 124)

⊙ **Game 2:** Bucketmania
⊙ **Cool-down and Review**

Practice 4

⊙ **Purpose:** To shoot free throws effectively
⊙ **Warm-up**
⊙ **Game 1:** On the Line (see page 131)
⊙ **Skill Practice:** Shooting free throws (see page 130)
⊙ **Game 2:** On the Line
⊙ **Cool-down and Review**

Practice 5

⊙ **Purpose:** To learn to set screens and execute pick-and-rolls
⊙ **Warm-up**
⊙ **Game 1:** Screen Door (see page 79)
⊙ **Skill Practice:** Setting screens (see page 79), pick-and-roll (see page 87)
⊙ **Game 2:** Pickin' for Points (see page 87)
⊙ **Cool-down and Review**

Practice 6

⊙ **Purpose:** To learn to defend against screens and pick-and-rolls
⊙ **Warm-up**
⊙ **Game 1:** Cut Off at the Pass (see page 95)
⊙ **Skill Practice:** Defending against screens (see page 95)
⊙ **Game 2:** Helping Hands (see page 99)
⊙ **Cool-down and Review**

Practice 7

⊙ **Purpose:** To learn to use the power dribble in attacking the basket
⊙ **Warm-up**
⊙ **Game 1:** In My Dust (see page 114)
⊙ **Skill Practice:** Power dribble (see page 110)
⊙ **Game 2:** In My Dust
⊙ **Cool-down and Review**

Practice 8

- ⊚ **Purpose:** To practice proper rebounding technique
- ⊚ **Warm-up**
- ⊚ **Game 1:** Cleaning the Glass (see page 137)
- ⊚ **Skill Practice:** Rebounding (see page 134)
- ⊚ **Game 2:** Cleaning the Glass
- ⊚ **Cool-down and Review**

Practice 9

- ⊚ **Purpose:** To learn how to create passing lanes
- ⊚ **Warm-up**
- ⊚ **Game 1:** Room to Move (see page 77)
- ⊚ **Skill Practice:** Creating passing lanes (see page 78)
- ⊚ **Game 2:** Room to Move
- ⊚ **Cool-down and Review**

Practice 10

- ⊚ **Purpose:** To learn how to cut off passing lanes
- ⊚ **Warm-up**
- ⊚ **Game 1:** No Passing Zone (see page 97)
- ⊚ **Skill Practice:** Cutting off passing lanes (see page 96) and helping out (see page 98)
- ⊚ **Game 2:** Helping Hands (see page 99)
- ⊚ **Cool-down and Review**

Practice 11

- ⊚ **Purpose:** To practice playing effective team offense
- ⊚ **Warm-up**
- ⊚ **Game 1:** Return to Sender (see page 85)
- ⊚ **Skill Practice:** Give-and-go (see page 85), creating passing lanes (see page 78), inbounds plays
- ⊚ **Game 2:** Room to Move (see page 77) or 5 Seconds to Go (see page 89)
- ⊚ **Cool-down and Review**

Practice 12

- ◎ **Purpose:** To practice playing effective team defense
- ◎ **Warm-up**
- ◎ **Game 1:** Pickin' Pockets (see page 87)
- ◎ **Skill Practice:** Cutting off passing lanes (see page 96), helping out (see page 98), playing on the ball and off the ball defense (see page 138)
- ◎ **Game 2:** Pickin' Pockets or Helping Hands (see page 140 or 99) or No Passing Zone (see page 97)
- ◎ **Cool-down and Review**

Practice 13

- ◎ **Purpose:** To learn to use fast breaks in attacking the basket
- ◎ **Warm-up**
- ◎ **Game 1:** Life in the Fast Lane (see page 82)
- ◎ **Skill Practice:** Transition game (see page 81)
- ◎ **Game 2:** Life in the Fast Lane
- ◎ **Cool-down and Review**

Practice 14

- ◎ **Purpose:** To practice proper rebounding technique
- ◎ **Warm-up**
- ◎ **Game 1:** Cleaning the Glass (see page 137)
- ◎ **Skill Practice:** Rebounding (see page 134)
- ◎ **Game 2:** Cleaning the Glass
- ◎ **Cool-down and Review**